STITCHED

25 years later,

I decided to put the record straight...

A TRUE ACCOUNT /

A MISCARRIAGE OF JUSTICE CASE /

DALE BRENDAN HYDE

/////// /////// /////// /////// /////// /////// /////// /////// /////// /////// /////// //////// /////// 'JUSTICE DENIED ANYWHERE // DIMINISHES JUSTICE EVERYWHERE' Martin Luther King Jnr. /////// /////// /////// /////// /////// /////// /////// /////// ///////

Verso page

Edit by

Steven Webb Editing
Services

Boksburg, South Africa

Published by

GMGA Publishing

ISBN: 9798704690221

He said, "In the midst of hate, I found there was, within me, an invincible love. In the midst of tears, I found there was, within me, an invincible smile. In the midst of chaos, I found there was, within me, an invincible calm. I realised, through it all, that in the midst of winter, I found there was, within me, an invincible summer. And that makes me happy. For it says that no matter how hard the world pushes against me, there's something stronger- something better, pushing right back."

For my Mother & Father,

With Love & appreciation for

Their genetic fingerprint

&

For my son, don't listen to
rumours, this is the real truth of
the matter. Love you.

&

For Gina

Dale Brendan Hyde V
Regina/vagina

VIEWING THE CASE AS A WHOLE, THERE WERE MANY FACTORS WHICH CAST SERIOUS DOUBT ON THE TRUTH OF MISS LEGALLY ANONYMOUS'S ACCOUNT.

ROYAL COURTS OF JUSTICE

HIGH COURT JUDGE LORD STAUGHTON

IN ALL MY CAREER IN LAW, I'VE ONLY EVER COME ACROSS 2 MISCARRIAGE OF JUSTICE CASES. THIS IS ONE OF THEM.

HIGH COURT JUDGE

RODNEY MELLOR MAPLES JAMESON

Foreword

by

Stephen 'The Devil' French.

The Female Weaponisation of Rape.

I was officially declared a "Target Criminal" by law enforcement agencies throughout the U. K. in the eighties and nineties. "The Devil", that was my nickname during my time involved in organised crime, which Graham Johnson relates in his bestselling book published in 2007. So, when Dale Brendan Hyde asked me to write this foreword, I saw it as a bit of a conundrum. How could I hope to explain with complete candour about being falsely accused of rape or being 'STITCHED'?

The act of Rape is a crime of sexual violence. Rape leaves the victims of this heinous crime totally devastated on so many levels. The physical damage is accompanied by serious psychological trauma. Violence Against Women and Girls (VAWG) is a serious problem in society today. This is an issue with an exceedingly high priority on the social and geopolitical agenda. But I wish to mention an issue that we, as men face. This is a crime, that in its psychological trauma, is worse than Rape. It's a crime committed by women against men and against other women, but for two different reasons. It is a crime that goes unpunished, mostly. This crime leaves its victims, and their family's lives in tatters. This is clear from the travesty of justice suffered by Dale Brendon Hyde, the author of this book.

We must bring this to people's attention because it is happening all too often and too many innocent men are being "STITCHED" by vindictive females. The reason the authorities claim they don't like to pursue and prosecute women who cry rape for cash or revenge is they maintain that it will discourage other victims of rape from coming forward? This perverse perspective is a nonsense notion because it allows almost no consideration for males falsely accused of the crime of rape.

They view men like us as collateral damage, and this is a flawed argument. What the authorities are trying to avoid, unwittingly promotes the opposite effect, and this is how by allowing these fraudulent accusers to go unpunished, it makes it so much harder for the actual victims of rape. Because of individuals who lay false claims to the crime, actual victims find it virtually impossible for people to believe them. This, therefore, becomes a crime against other women who are the genuine victims of rape and battery, and not just the men falsely accused of the crime.

I believe there needs to be an amendment to the law to protect a man's identity from women who take part in such pernicious malicious false allegations.

Those of you reading who think the CPS do not withhold evidence that proves a defendant is innocent do not understand the extent of the malfeasance that is crippling the British Criminal Justice System. There were forty-seven prosecutions for rape or serious sexual offences cancelled in the first weeks of 2018 because of this unlawful conduct. There are serious "systemic problems" regarding disclosure, prompting calls for a wider inquiry into this behaviour. Considering the findings, the Criminal Bar Association (CBA) called for a much wider inquiry.

Dale Brendan Hyde served twenty-seven months of an eight year and three-month sentence before being acquitted of rape in the Appeals Court in London. Those twenty-seven months, however, are nothing to what he has had to endure for the past twenty-five years. The stigma around the word 'rape' has tormented him ever since. This is the story of how Hyde was 'STITCHED' by an unscrupulous woman, who never counted on the strength and determination of the man she laid false claim against, a man who risked his freedom to prove his innocence. This is his story.

Stephen French – Formerly known as "The Devil", now known as "The Fighting Preacher".

12 June 2020

Chapter 1

The dream was graphic and long into the night. She had moaned throughout the entire period of consenting intercourse. She had enjoyed it last week, just like the first time I had slept with her around three weeks earlier.

The dawn light crept through my Uncle Roland's spare bedroom window, where I had made my home for the last few months. The dream seemed over, yet the crashing sound of disturbing noise was hard to pinpoint. Dreams transcended from one nonsensical stream into another, yet right at that moment I knew my dream had become something that only nightmares can conjure into the mind.

"Get out of bed you filthy rapist bastard!"

Protocol had flown out of the window from the first out of breath copper who, as I awoke, was pulling my duvet away from my naked body. I awoke fully as the sounds of multiple heavy boots thundered up the stairway and seemed to bulge into my flimsy doorway that separated what had been my normal life, from the one that now awaited me. His screaming words didn't register. Mouths contorting in angry ways, conveying information that I felt sure couldn't be for my ears.

It was only a small bedroom, tucked away at the back of the house on Grantley Street and with about seven burly men now crowding my bed space, the room shrank into what felt like a cell. I could see a few uniformed coppers through my blinking tired eyes cramming into the back of the bunch. A serious-looking detective dressed in normal attire was now telling me to get some clothes on. I recall asking just what the hell all this interruption was about. The words that the first copper had screamed at me just didn't register, and I was looking for this bloke who I took to be in charge to tell me just what it was all about. Again I was told that I was under arrest for rape and that I needed to hurry and get some clothes on and that they would explain everything down at the station on Wood Street.

I searched around to find something to wear. My clothes from the previous night were slung over a chair in the corner. So, I pulled a green and white Benetton t-shirt over my head, followed by a Joe Casely-Hayford knitted jumper. I then pulled on a pair of dark, denim Destroy jeans and laced up a pair of Deakin boots. They then lead me down the dark narrow stairs which brought us out into the back kitchen. Halfway down the stairs, I heard more commotion and shouting. There was a little sliding door that separated the kitchen from the stairs. As they bundled me through the doorway, I noticed my uncle on the floor. This fat copper was holding him down with his arm up his back while another copper in uniform knelt beside him, trying to calm him down.

"No way, no way." These were the first words I heard from my uncle's mouth. I could see behind the thick lenses of his glasses he was in floods of tears and upset. I shouted at the fat copper to get the fuck off him, while they both tried to calm my uncle on the floor, telling him to relax and that it would all get sorted down at the station.

As some other coppers cuffed me behind my back, I tried to reassure my uncle they had it all wrong and that I would be back soon. The seriousness of the bullshit charge made me ask him to make sure he phoned my mum and to get her to call a solicitor. They bundled me out through the back door while all I could hear was my Uncle Roland shouting after the coppers.

"He doesn't need to rape anyone!"

"He's got more birds after him than you can shake a stick at!"

"He's not like that!"

"He would never do a thing like that!"

I wouldn't see my uncle or that house again for a very long time.

Chapter 2

I had been in trouble before with the police, yet it had been a good while ago and not for any kind of sexual crime. Yet I still felt the embarrassment rise inside of me as they brought me from the back kitchen door and up through the small garden path and out onto the street out front. It surprised me to see just how many police cars they had parked out front, with a few Black Mariah vans over on the other kerb. Several uniformed coppers steered me toward one van until a detective shouted over and said,

"Bring him over and put him in the back of the car."

As the door slammed hard, the silence in the back seat engulfed my mind. I knew the dreaming was over. I knew this was wide awake reality. Yet I felt like I couldn't catch my breath. In my attempts to calm myself, I just kept repeating over and over that they were making a huge mistake, and that I had nothing to worry about as I'd done nothing wrong. With all the commotion it was surprising the whole street had not woken up, but all I noticed as the car pulled away was my uncle's neighbour and friend, Ronnie Crook, looking out of his front room window as I was driven away.

The journey from Grantley Street towards Wood Street police station was familiar. I stared out of the car window at empty streets, though. The time was around 6 a.m. No one spoke in the car on the brief journey up through the back streets of the city. We pulled onto Wood Street, and halfway down the car did a left turn through the electric gates that allowed entry into the back cell block compound. As the gates slowly whirled open, I still couldn't quite believe I was being transferred through.

It's hard to recall all the details, as I'm writing now some twenty-five years later. I remember clearly though, that as they pushed me forward through the doors and towards the main booking desk where the sergeant stood scowling at me, there was a white pull down board listing in different colours who was in custody and for what alleged crime. It also listed dates of arrest, solicitor names and other information. With one name stating that the poor kid was on suicide watch.

Now all that information was irrelevant to me at that point. Upon my entry to the custody suite, the sergeant's assistant quickly pulled down the board so I couldn't read the top few names. I was then searched and booked in, giving my details. Again the absurdity of the situation hit me as the sergeant, after listening to my details, sauntered over to the whiteboard and wrote my name and the word RAPE. I just stared at the word in disbelief and felt like someone hypnotised me before a copper pulled me away from the desk by my jumper sleeve to march me up the long corridor. Outside this steel cell door, he told me to remove my boots and belt before placing me in the cell.

The slam of the door had me wide awake now as I stared around the empty concrete box. On the wall in spray painted stencil capitals, I noticed that some

17

prisoner before me had scratched out the letter 'D' on what should have read,

'IF YOU HAVE A PROBLEM WITH DRUGS CONTACT THE STAFF IN CHARGE FOR ADVICE.'

It was the first time I had smiled since waking up that morning. I paced the cell floor, wondering if I had a problem with RUGS? For what seemed at least an hour, no one came near my cell door. Then it opened, and two detectives stood in the open doorway and informed me that my solicitor had arrived.

I led the way back along the corridor towards the custody desk where a Mr John Batty waited. I didn't know him from Adam yet found some small comfort in his name. My mother's maiden name had been Batty. He seemed a nice enough chap upon first impressions, and I was desperate to speak with him away from the coppers, to spill my thoughts about this wrongful arrest. In a side room away from the large custody desk, we eventually got to speak.

Again, I don't recall the exact conversation, but I remember him saying to me that this was a very serious situation and that he was glad he was there to help. He explained that he was just the duty solicitor for that day and that if I wished to appoint someone else to represent me in my forthcoming interview, then I was more than welcome to do so. When he explained he was from Williams Solicitors firm, I relaxed a little. Edward, who worked at the firm, had been the boyfriend to the mother of my best friend when I was in middle school. So I knew of Edward a little, which made me think fate had sent the right man in John Batty to my rescue. Looking back, I realised this was a mistake and the lack of backbone or honesty from this team would cost me dearly in the long run.

I spilled my guts to Mr Batty about how they had got this whole arrest very wrong. They had still not given me any details about who they were saying I had allegedly raped. I knew one thing for sure, though, I had raped no one. And that they were barking up the wrong tree on this matter. John Batty listened and tried to interrupt me to reassure me that everything would be sorted out as soon as the police conducted their interview. They then took me and put me back in my cell to await this part of the procedure.

Pacing again, I did my best to keep from worrying about the seriousness of the situation. My instinct telling me I had nothing to fear as I had done nothing worth being charged for and that whatever terrible mistake this all was, they would soon realise their error and I would soon be back home. I recall I had plans for the weekend, as the day of the arrest was a Saturday morning, and I was sure in my heart I would be out to enjoy my weekend as normal. I wouldn't enjoy a weekend out again for a very long time.

The interview was about to begin. Mr Batty sat to my right on our side of the table, while two detectives sat opposite. A large file was in front of them on the desk. They allowed me a plastic cup of water, to loosen my tongue, probably. The police turned on the recorder in the room and this little red light came on. They were now ready to get things underway.

When they started reading out the charge and statement, I interrupted saying this was all bullshit and I didn't want to listen to any more lies. Mr Batty advised me to just let them get through what they had to say, and then it would be my turn to reply to the allegations. So I sat there feeling rather uncomfortable as I listened to them describe some horrific rape scenario that made little sense to me regarding my involvement.

The only thing familiar in the story was the name of this lass that I had slept with twice. Once, about a month ago and the second time around a week ago. Everything throughout these two encounters had been consenting and had nothing at all to do with rape.

I listened in horror at the blatant lies as the police read out to me and Mr Batty the full extent of her statement. After trying to get my head around it all, Mr Batty informed me I could make a "no reply" comment on everything. I chose to not go down that route as I had nothing at all to hide and I needed to clarify very clearly to the police just how wrong they had got all this and that this statement read out to me was a total pack of lies.

For several hours in that interview room, I did my best to set the record straight and inject some much needed truth into the equation. The police did the usual hard ball routine, and I could sense from the off that they honestly believed her statement and that it was only a matter of time before I broke down and confessed. That would never happen in a million years. The bullshit I was listening to outraged me, and the in-depth statement that **MISS LEGALLY ANONYMOUS** had given disturbed me.

Chapter 3

For me, this nightmare started on a Sunday teatime. I had been on the front doorstep of my Uncle Roland's house on Grantley Street, just having a look outside and catching some fresh air, when I noticed a lad I knew from school walking down the road. The RAT shouted a greeting from the other side, and I said hello back. He then walked over, and we talked about nothing in particular. I recall him saying how bored he was and had no plans for the evening and did I fancy meeting up in the city for a few pints later?

Nothing crazy, just a Sunday night and a few drinks around a few of the city's many drinking establishments. I remember not being that bothered about going out as I'd been out the night before, but the RAT persisted with his invite. I said okay and that I would meet him in the Patio Bar around 8 p.m. In hindsight, if I had known where this night out would lead, I would have barricaded myself in my uncle's house and never spoken to the Rat again. Rat was how I would come to refer to my soon to be co accused, and it was a name well suited.

After a nice bath, I sorted out my long, curly, black hair and put on some nice designer clothes and left the house around half past seven in the evening. I exited the deserted subway onto the bottom of The Springs and cut through by the side of the Cathedral and walked a little further up towards the main entrance to the Ridings Shopping Centre. It was just inside the mall and down the escalators to the right where the Patio Bar was located. I didn't take that entrance because there was a back door to the right just before you entered the Ridings.

The Patio Bar was a nice little place where many people would meet up to start their night out. It was quiet as I bought a bottle of lager and waited for the Rat. He entered down the same back stairs I had just before 8 p.m. We rinsed off a few bottles of lager and moved on to find a busier bar up at the top of Westgate. In 1994, Westgate was always busy, and this Sunday was no different. We moved around a few bars chatting to mates who we knew and a few of the single ladies out looking for a dance before the dreaded Monday morning alarm awakened them back to work.

We eventually landed in Bitz Nightclub, which was a bar that used to be the first bank in Wakefield. It also had the moniker of having the record for the longest bar in the country. We were right at the back where the dance floor was, just watching the ladies bust some moves. We had chatted a few girls up that night, but we didn't want to buy them drinks all night and stick with them to see if they fancied a night back at theirs. I know it sounds loose, but we were young and good looking and only nineteen and twenty years old. A few one-night stands were the order of the day back then.

Through the flashing strobe lights of the dance floor I noticed two girls approaching, and I recognised one because of her long blonde dreaded hair. The reason I recognised her was because around three weeks earlier I had bumped into her and ended up going back to her house in the early evening and sleeping with her. For me, it had just been a chance encounter that had led to some casual sex. In my mind, I'd had no intention of seeing her again or getting into anything like a relationship.

To be honest, I had forgotten about the encounter and wouldn't have given it another moment's thought until I had her stood in front of me in Bitz with her friend. The one thing that was very important though to my first encounter with **MISS LEGALLY ANONYMOUS**, was when I had left her house three weeks earlier she had given me a lock of braided hair and tied it to my wrist. It wasn't something I would normally wear, but after sleeping with her, I allowed her to tie it onto my wrist. It stayed on for a few days until it unravelled, and I just removed it. I kept it though, and I remember the day after I had slept with her my mother had noticed it when I went to visit her in Alverthorpe, and I'd told her a girl I'd slept with named **MISS LEGALLY ANONYMOUS** had given it to me. This minor detail would be significant later during the trial at Leeds Crown Court.

Back in Bitz Nightclub, we had spoken to the pair of them, just flirting and asking mundane questions, trying to feign some interest in the pair of them. They were definitely not model types. After a drink, we were about to move on and go find another bar. **MISS LEGALLY ANONYMOUS** sensed we were about to go and she suggested, in front of her friend Miss Green, that if we didn't end up with any plans later, then we were welcome to come down to her house for a nightcap.

She didn't give either of us her address, as she knew that I already knew where she lived. I think she may have just told me the door number as I was leaving, so I didn't get confused on the street if we went down. She also said, in a joking manner, that if we got down to hers and she wasn't back that we might try the back window. We just laughed that odd statement off and left.

Leaving Bitz we had no intention of going down, as we expected to pull a few nicer looking ladies in the next bar. It turned out though that the few girls we did chat with after leaving Bitz seemed too much like hard work, and by the end of the night we got some food and decided why the hell not go down for a drink and a laugh. I had told the Rat I had already slept with the blonde one and I guess in our young minds we thought she would be up for some fun. But we didn't think it would involve both of us. In my mind I thought it would be only me that would get off with her, as I had been there before only weeks earlier.

We walked down Westgate and then took the back lane along the side of the maximum security prison and took a shortcut over some playing fields until we made it to where **MISS LEGALLY ANONYMOUS** lived. The time was somewhere around one am. We knocked on the front door and received no answer. So we waited a few minutes and then knocked again, thinking maybe she had not got home yet. We waited a while, seeing as though we had taken the effort to walk down.

A light rain was falling, so we moved to the back of the house to shelter. The Rat noticed that the only thing that covered the kitchen window was a piece of plyboard, which was just lent up against the ledge. It wasn't fastened to the window at all. As the rain fell harder, it was getting colder, so the Rat suggested we just get in through the open window and at least wait in the house where it was dry. We now knew what she had meant when she had said try the back window.

Now this might not have been a clever thing to do. It wasn't right. But how the prosecution later twisted it and used it in court was just a disgrace. I accept then, and even more so now, all these years later that it was the wrong thing to do, but my hand on my heart, we did it in all innocence and it had even been suggested in a roundabout way by **MISS LEGALLY ANONYMOUS** herself as we had left Bitz nightclub.

Once we had climbed into the kitchen, the Rat opened the fridge, more to illuminate the room as we didn't know where the lights were. There were a few cans of beer in the fridge and we got one each, thinking she wouldn't mind. Once we had got our bearings a little more, I remembered the layout and led the way through the kitchen door and went to wait for her to return home while sitting in the living room. We put a small lamp on and sat on the sofa chatting.

Fifteen minutes later we heard the key turn in the door and excited voices. **MISS LEGALLY ANONYMOUS** entered the room and without missing a beat said,

"Oh, you got in through the window then?" To which we just laughed and said,

"Yeah, sorry it was raining hard and we thought it would be okay to wait inside."

In the doorway just behind her was a woman who we didn't know. It wasn't the lass who had been with **MISS LEGALLY ANONYMOUS** in the Bitz nightclub. There was a conversation that went on between the two of them while we just sat on the sofa waiting for an introduction. **MISS LEGALLY ANONYMOUS** didn't introduce us though and after about two minutes her mate said she was leaving and we shouted: "See ya later", and the next thing we knew **MISS LEGALLY ANONYMOUS** was walking back into the front room saying her mates who had dropped her off in their car had gone home.

Later down the line, she gave a different account to the people who recorded her first statement, and again refuted line for line by her actual friends who she had called as prosecution witnesses to help back up her bullshit lies. I later found out that her friend had asked who we were, to which **MISS LEGALLY ANONYMOUS** had said,

"Oh it's okay, they are my mates."

Her friend said that having two strange men just waiting for **MISS LEGALLY ANONYMOUS** to return home had embarrassed her. Yet **MISS LEGALLY ANONYMOUS** had shown her the door and got rid of her as quickly as possible, saying not to worry, and everything was fine. Her friend had gone back to the car outside where another friend was in the driver's seat. They had waited outside for five minutes as they felt it was strange that she had wanted to get them out of the house so quick. But after waiting five minutes, thinking everything must be okay, which it was from our point of view, they had driven off home.

(Perfected Grounds of Appeal by Judge Rodney Jameson)

Page 9.

The scene at MISS LEGALLY ANONYMOUS'S home when she returned with two other women to find Hyde and THE RAT there. C. 1.15 a.m. 6th June.

MISS LEGALLY ANONYMOUS described herself as "mad": She said she had told Miss PINK that Hyde and THE RAT should not be there and that she was "quite mad".

Miss PINK said that MISS LEGALLY ANONYMOUS was embarrassed. She had referred to Hyde and THE RAT as "my mates", she clearly didn't want her and Miss Milson there and showed them the door.

Miss PURPLE said: "MISS LEGALLY ANONYMOUS was quite calm"; "It was quite clear that MISS LEGALLY ANONYMOUS did not want her at the house"; "She...sort of showed us the door."

Chapter 4

Twenty-five years later, as I write this, it is impossible to remember the exact way that the night unfolded. But I can say with a solid clarity that we all talked in the room for about fifteen minutes before **MISS LEGALLY ANONYMOUS** went and fetched us both a can of lager from the fridge. We sat and drank and talked some more. There was a rug in the middle of the floor which she sat on. From the chair I had been sitting in, I asked her to come towards me to talk a little more to me, while the Rat just laid back on the sofa chilling with his can.

I had already slept with her a few weeks before and we were merry from our night out, but we were not drunk. The flirting started. Before long we were kissing as I leaned forward from the chair while she leaned into me kneeling on the floor. I remember things getting a little heated and me moving my hands over her breasts through her top. Then both of us lifted her top over her head so I could play with her breasts in her bra. We knew the Rat was watching us, but it didn't bother her one bit.

I had my hands roaming around inside her bra and she moaned softly. She looked around to where the Rat was lounging and stared at him in lust. As she did this, the Rat pulled his designer jumper off over his head. Bare chested he laid back on the sofa while she turned her attention back to me. The kissing got more intense.

I removed her lace-up boots and peeled off her tight jeans, so she was just in her underwear now.

Then the Rat moved off the sofa, and they kissed each other while I undressed myself too. By the time I had removed my designer jumper and jeans, all three of us were down to our underwear. It was at this stage where **MISS LEGALLY ANONYMOUS** suggested we carry the action on upstairs in her bedroom. So we let her lead the way upstairs. Her bedroom was how I remembered it from last time I had been in there. It was an untidy mess of clothes thrown all over the floor and surfaces covered with makeup and junk.

The Rat went and sat in a chair in the corner to the left-hand side of the bed while me and **MISS LEGALLY ANONYMOUS** lay down on the bed and started kissing again. Within five minutes I was having sex with her and she was moaning in pleasure throughout until we both climaxed. She then laid there for a few minutes having a breather and then got on all fours with her invite clear to the Rat. He needed no more encouragement and was soon deep inside her from behind.

I remember a strange thing happening while he was having sex with her, as he stopped and said he was bleeding somewhere around his penis. I just thought at that point that she had got her period at a really awkward time. But she hadn't and somehow he had cut his penis. Now it wasn't from doing anything rough, as he had—from my viewpoint— only had casual sex with her from behind. He wasn't being forceful or anything like that. He got up and took himself off to the bathroom to clean himself. While he was gone she played with me again, getting me hard.

By the time the Rat came back into the bedroom **MISS LEGALLY ANONYMOUS** was giving me oral sex on all fours and the Rat just got back in behind her and carried on where he had left off, with her sucking me while he thrust into her. He finished himself off to orgasm, and I let her suck me some more after he had pulled out and lounged back into the chair at the left-hand side of the bed.

After a few minutes she seemed to lose enthusiasm for the oral, and to be fair I had no more enthusiasm and the whole sex session just ended. I think the Rat rolled and lit a cigarette, while I just lay on the bed for a while talking to her. About ten minutes later, she asked us if we were hungry or wanted a cup of tea. The time would have been around 3 a.m. I think. We both said we would have a brew, and she said she would make us some toast to go with it. She disappeared off down the stairs, leaving us both to get dressed into our underwear again.

When we heard her shout up the stairs that the toast was ready, we went down to the lounge and got the rest of our clothes back on. She brought two cups of tea and a large plate full of buttered toast into the room. We sat eating the toast and sipping our mugs of tea while she got her jeans and top off the floor and dressed again. After finishing our food and drink we got ready to make our way home. We would head back towards the city and the subway , where I could turn left onto Grantley Street and the Rat could carry on to his mum's house where he lived.

At the front door we said our goodbyes and said we should meet up again sometime. **MISS**

LEGALLY ANONYMOUS agreed to this, and we left her one of our mobile phone numbers. I can't recall if it was mine or the Rat's number she got. Looking back in hindsight to what rubbish she came out with in her statements though, it all changed depending on who she was talking to. These weren't the actions of brutal, sadistic rapists. Oh, thanks for the rape love, here's our phone number!

Again, you must ask yourself that with her having the main door key in the lock the whole time, then if she was brutally raped like she claimed, why did she not walk out of the house while we were both upstairs in her bedroom? But no, it was cups of tea all round with a plate of toast and a mobile to call us again on the way out.

(Perfected Grounds of Appeal by Judge Rodney Jameson)

<u>**Page 17. Actions of Hyde between alleged rape and arrest.**</u>

1. **Before leaving MISS LEGALLY ANONYMOUS'S HOME. She was given a telephone number so that she could contact the defendants again.**

Chapter 5

The rain had stopped, thankfully, as we retraced our original path from her home back to where we had come from.

Just near where Mr Parker's newsagent is located was where the entrance to the subway used to be. Just near the old baths on Sun Lane. There was one of those old police box buildings opposite the newsagent with a little wall in front. The Rat sat down to roll a smoke. I took a pew myself and was minding my business when I noticed a uniformed copper walking towards us. He was friendly enough and in a joking kind of manner said to us both.

"What you two lads up to at this time of night?"

I guess the time was around 4 a.m. The copper sat down beside us while the Rat lit his smoke. We said, laughing to him in reply to his questions, that he wouldn't believe us if we told him, to which he had replied, "try me".

"We have just had three in a bed sex with a girl down (I won't mention the estate, but it was the same one the lass we had just left lived on)!"

The copper noted this in his little notebook. He wrote down our full names and addresses. He checked that there were no warrants out for our arrest and that we had not escaped from prison. His checks came back fine, and he said goodnight and told us to get ourselves home and get some rest.

I'd like to thank PC Ward for at least trying to help us with his statement, which he read out in court, and for not being corrupted after being advised by the senior detective, DET MC DX, to alter his opinion on matters that night. DET MC DX had told PC Ward that just because he had written little in his notebook, he could still say anything to the court.

After the subway, I'd turned left onto Grantley St. while the Rat carried on walking home. We said night to each other and parted company. A few days later we met again by chance at a flat on Westgate, which was above the then Rooftop Gardens Nightclub. A mutual friend lived there, and there were a few other lads in the flat. The Rat had been bragging about our threesome sex with this lass **MISS LEGALLY ANONYMOUS**, and somehow we ended up agreeing to go down again and see if she was up for some more fun. The other lads were heading elsewhere and were going to pass this estate anyway, so we walked down together.

Shouting to be let in, that was what **MISS LEGALLY ANONYMOUS** says we were doing once we got outside her house. We may have raised our voices, but that was only because we hadn't entered past her garden gate and she had only opened her front room window to speak to us. Yes, we had asked if we could come in, and her friend from the nightclub Miss Green was in her house too, and they said no.

That was not a problem, and we left, with me and the RAT heading back towards the city centre and Westgate while the other few lads that had been with us went on their way somewhere else around the estate. I didn't think about any of this again until a week later when I was in Wood Street police station under arrest for rape.

It's hard to remember the sequence in which I voluntarily gave interviews to the police while in custody. On the second day, they told me they also had the RAT in custody, which I kind of figured they would anyway if the allegation involved that night we slept with **MISS LEGALLY ANONYMOUS**. I remember on the second day they told me that our separate interviews 'conveniently' matched and that our stories were much the same. I remember feeling annoyed that they were putting this across as if we had concocted some alibi instead of the more obvious conclusion, which was that we were both telling the truth.

{Perfected Grounds of Appeal by Judge Rodney Jameson}

Hyde co-operated fully in police interview, giving a detailed account, consistent in detail with his evidence at trial.

It was like this from when they first locked us up. No one seemed to believe a word of anything I was saying, and I couldn't understand why.

The Sunday night they charged us both with a crime I vehemently denied and a crime I felt passionately about as something I hated to my very core. I'm the same as most people, I hate rape and despise vile humans who commit this horrendous crime. To feel I was now being judged as someone who did this despicable act was sickening to my stomach. I still felt that they would soon come to my cell door saying, "Sorry we have got it all wrong," and that I was free to go. But it just never happened. They informed me I would go up in front of the magistrate at Wakefield on Monday morning. Now that they had interviewed and charged both of us, we could share a cell until the courts opened. If we wanted food ordered from anywhere, they would sort it if we paid.

Obviously, we agreed to share a cell, and they brought the Rat to mine, and the door slammed shut. Again, all these years later it's hard to recall what we said at that point, but I remember we were both shocked at our arrests and both confident that the magistrate would grant us bail, at least until we could sort out this terrible mistake. One thing in hindsight was that the Rat had a terrible secret which he kept from me. Well, in fact, it's something he kept from me for many years until I read something about him in the paper. It puts a strange angle on this entire story, but I will get to that later down the line.

At this point, I knew we were both innocent of raping **MISS LEGALLY ANONYMOUS,** and I felt sorry for the Rat as we were both in a very difficult predicament.

The police allowed us to use the cash in our accounts to pay for our order of a mixed kebab each, which seemed surreal as they arrived at the cell door, and we tucked in to what would become our last fast food meal for a very long time.

As morning broke, I woke to the sounds of buzzers and walkie talkies and slams of hard steel doors. They opened us up and led us down the corridor to wash and to brush our teeth. They gave me this metal toothbrush that cut my gums and a bar of cheap soap. I cleaned myself up the best I could and tried to rid my body and clothes of that distinct stink of grubby police cells.

In the old days, the cells at Wood Street had an underground tunnel that led under the road which brought you up into the magistrate's cells. They had stopped transporting prisoners that way some time ago, so we waited for the Group Four bus to arrive at the front of the nick. They cuffed us separately and walked us out to be banged up tight in the back of the bus's small, plastic cubicles to ride less than one minute around the corner to the magistrate cell door entrance.

I will always remember this old gaoler from the courts being decent to me that morning, while the rest of the people in authority I met had an attitude that I could only conclude came from the stigma attached to the word rape. It was a stigma that would never leave my side.

It was just before lunch when they called us up into the courtroom and I tried to take in the faces that were all staring at us. My mum's worried face stared out at me from the public benches and I gave her my best reassuring smile.

I expected nothing more than to get bail and to go home, but soon found out that this would not be the case. It was a short informal hearing with the three magistrates doing the worst job ever in their entire careers as they remanded two innocent young men, one still a teenager, into the custody of the prison system!

In total disbelief, they led me back down to the old dungeon cells to await the prison bus for HMP Moorland in Doncaster, which was the nearest remand spot for young offenders. I think around four p.m. the noise of the van's reverse warning buzzer backing down the narrow side street outside the court cells was the signal to get ready to board. They handed us over into the custody of the Group Four guards, cuffed us and placed us in the van. I began to panic, with my mind spinning with just how out-of-control things were getting. There was also the dreaded thought of entering prison with a charge of such a vile nature. I knew only too well from my previous sentence for the robbery that I had committed and served my rightful time for, just how they viewed rapists behind bars. And it wasn't a good thing. I had despised them on my robbery sentence, and along with the rest of the lads had tried my best to make their lives a living hell. So, I had quite a daunting feeling as the van sped off towards Doncaster. I looked out of the tiny window at my city and thought about when I would be free, walking my streets again.

The thing is, with a miscarriage of justice, they treat you as if you have committed a crime, but you haven't and it's hard to get your head around the many stages of incarceration. To be spoken to by people who hated your guts because of the nature of the crime, was hard to deal with, and still is to this very day. As I've stated the stigma has never gone, and in the latter part of the book I will mention how people have treated me just as bad on the outside as they treated me on the inside.

The last time I had been in HMP Moorland was a few years earlier and nothing except my charge had changed, and also the fact I was now being booked into the prison reception for nothing more than sleeping with some girl on a quiet Sunday night a week before.

The word surreal doesn't come close. After we gave all our details, they allocated me my new prison number. Again, the contrast in experiences from my previous trip inside couldn't have been more different. The first time I had gone to prison, I had laughed when the guard had given me my number of JR1 007. Most of the time you only use your last three digits, it filled my entire sentence with laughs when they asked, and I gave the James Bond theme 007 answer. This time my number, which I didn't deserve, was to be FPO 472. The Rat who had gone before me at the reception desk was FPO 471.

Neither number will I ever forget, and for different reasons.

Chapter 6

I think it took about all of ten minutes before some wise-arse asked the Rat what he was in for and he had said in quite an aggressive reply, "Rape, why!" I remember coming towards this stocky lad dressed in the prison kitchen whites and telling him to fuck off away or else. They then put us back in this glass fronted waiting room until they took us onto one of the wings. They had called the principal officer because of our charges and he had taken us to one side and told us he recommended going on the protection wing, but it was our choice. We went straight into a normal wing and took our chances.

I need you to understand, trying to remember back over twenty-five years I need a little poetic licence, but they placed us in a cell together, and a few prisoners on jobs that allowed them to roam a little, came to our cell door. Some knew the Rat, because he had come out of prison not too long ago for glassing a lad in the face and had served some time up in Deerbolt Castle as a youth of sixteen. So, we were no angels or naïve when it came to getting on in prison. It was the one thing that saved us, really. I cannot begin to imagine coming through the system with a false rape charge up your arse and never having been one to tread the landings before.

We were both down the block within the first few days for fighting! It had been the next day, and they had announced lunch. A screw opened our cell door, and we walked towards the big hall, where at the far end was a row of metal hotplates where the server lads dished out the grub. I can't remember whether it was me or the Rat who had said at one station he was down as vegetarian and that he wanted the last piece of fish on this tray. The big con had eyed it up for his own grub later when they had finished dishing out the food, and he wasn't thrilled about this new con in front of him going on about being a vegetarian and wanting the fish. In prison, arguments flare up over the slightest of things. This server lad had tried to tell us to move on and put something else on our plates. I know only that in the ensuing violence, the server con got cracked around his mouth with the edge of the metal food tray and then all the screws were running at full speed towards us and we went under in the scrum.

Down the block about half hour later my cell door opened, and I got ready to fight again. Instead, there was a friendly faced screw standing there with some pizza from the Rat's brother, J, over in the adult prison opposite, which was HMP Lindholme. So I ate my lunch in peace for that day. I should have been free, though, to walk into Pizza Hut and order whatever I fancied!

Back up from the block, we settled the best we could into life on the wing. The kick-off in the dining room had proved to the wannabe bullies that we would be well up for violence and we were not the dodgy looking types. I remember getting on the phones and speaking with family and a few close friends, explaining just what the hell had gone off.

Everyone I spoke to was shocked and upset. My dad was out as usual working in the Middle East, so I'd not been able to get a word out to him, but my mum and sister had spoken to him. My grandma on my mum's side was devastated and praying every single night for me. It was things like this that people didn't understand, the impact on everyone who cared about me, the doubt of such a stigmatic word as rape. They knew I'd not done something like this, but it was hot gossip, and I could only imagine how difficult it was for my mum on the village lane or my little sister at high school. It was what kept me awake at night in my cell, furious with the lies from this little tart that had put me into false remand.

The solicitors were trying their best to calm me and reassure me they were moving as fast as they could and were going for bail at the next magistrate hearing, which was about two weeks away. So all we could do was try to get on the best we could in prison. Watching paint dry is a common expression, but this was something else. The time just dragged on and I tried to sleep away most of the days just hoping to wake up in my bed at home and not to be in this living nightmare. But that never happened, and every time I blinked my eyes open and noticed the cell wall, my heart would sink, and depression was rearing its ugly head at the desperation of the situation I was in.

Now, like I stated earlier, I believed my solicitors were doing everything they could for me. But in hindsight some twenty-five years later, I realise they must have known certain things about this bullshit charge and the facts surrounding it they never told me about, ever!

If they and the police had been more upfront about everything they knew about the Rat, then I don't think I would ever have been charged and had to go through this miscarriage of justice. There are a few things like the trial, time served, and getting acquitted to reveal first before I go into detail about the Rat's little secret.

The day for court eventually arrived, and we went through the painstaking rigmarole needed to get you from your cell and onto the Group Four bus. It was great to see the outside world again after being banged up for a long fortnight for nothing and I felt confident again that this time the courts had heard and read a little more about the case, so they could bail us to wait on the outside while they cleared up this obvious mess.

The familiarity of Wakefield gave mc a much needed confidence boost as the van turned into the narrow street where the magistrate court was situated. We were once again led into the side door where the cells were and banged up to wait our call up in front of the beak.

It was late afternoon before we got our slot and the wait in those old grubby court dungeon cells had been one long bore. All eyes were upon us again as we entered up the stairs and into the courtroom, cuffed to two screws.

The hearing was long and my solicitor, Mr Batty, tried to argue the case that this was a dispute between consent and that it would be safe and right to allow bail until the facts came to light in a higher court. The stigmatic sounds of the charge blinded the stupid bastard magistrates as they bandied the word rape around the four walls. I felt like I was in some kind of weird stage play that had nothing to do with me until again I heard the words from the main beak in the middle of the bench who said,

"Remanded into custody!"

Dejected, I traipsed down the stairs and back into the cell to wait to speak to my solicitor who they had informed me would be down soon to speak to me. When he got down there and they unlocked me, we went into a side room that had no door and spoke about why they had denied bail. I remember him saying how he couldn't understand it and that he was really sorry. But the fact of the matter was I would go back on the Group Four van to HMP Moorland, to wait for, I think it was going to be three weeks they had said, until I could try for bail through a judge in chambers.

The one thing that stands out so clear to this day, is that while waiting in the magistrate's dungeons, a few other prisoners had entered the cell and gone up at different times for their own cases. We had not spoken to them all, but one lad we spoke to about the case had said something to us we couldn't believe.

He himself had slept with **MISS LEGALLY ANONYMOUS**, and had also let himself into the house via this boarded-up back window, clearly stating that she had asked him to get in that way if she wasn't home, just like she had told us that night in her joking way. A way now, that was being used in her statement to make out we had broken in and were waiting there like animals to rape her. It's just ludicrous. And looking back now, I'm sure we told the solicitors what we had heard from the lad in the cells. So I'm at a loss why they didn't take a statement for it. But looking back as a 46-year-old man, it seems I would have done a lot of things differently than when I was just a scared 20-year-old kid with the weight of the world on his shoulders and not thinking straight or knowing much about the law.

John Batty was not giving me any confidence at all. But he kept saying that his firm had excellent barristers, so I stuck with them because of this. Maybe, had I been advised and represented by a better solicitor in the beginning, I wouldn't have needed a firm with great barristers. But again, looking back in hindsight, no solicitor could have stopped these crooked wheels of justice from rolling over my life in such a hurtful way.

Maybe John Batty knew of the Rat's secret. He must have done. They all piss in the same pot and drink in the same pubs and chat on the circuit. There is no way that he wasn't privy to the information that I wouldn't know for another thirteen years. Surely, his boss Edward must have known as the owner of the firm representing me. The police who were handling the case knew of the Rat's secret. So why didn't anyone tell me, an innocent young lad of twenty-years-old who was being put through such a traumatic ordeal!

Looking back, the entire case stank to high heaven. It stunk then, and its stench is overpowering now as a forty-six-year-old man looking back. They probably didn't think twenty-five years later I would open up this can of rotten worms. Well, I have, and I still want answers and justice. I want the police complaints commissioner to reopen the case and investigate this joke.

Back in the prison cell at Moorland, I settled down the best I could to await the judge-in-chamber's hearing. Time hung inside the clock as if all its mechanisms had broken. The four walls play tricks with the mind, and I guarded my sanity. I won't bore you, the reader, with the mundane monotony of prison life; most will understand and get the picture. The cell is bare, with rotting paint, peeling walls, a high up bar with pigeon shit caked all over it. A bunk bed that would break your back with its lumpy discomfort. The itchy green blankets that smelled of years old foist. The noise of banging and shouting, which sometimes they would direct at us yelling,

"Rapist rapists, hang hang em, hang hang em!" When we were bothered we would try to find out which idiot was giving it the big one out of the cell windows by yelling,
"Fuckin' come to my cell at unlock and say that to my face!"

No one did. But even so, the stigma and sly cruelty was enough to affect me in there, and it made me paranoid. I almost forgot to mention the minor riots breaking out all over the prison. Our toilet and sink got smashed up, and the bedding set on fire and slung out of the bars to burn with the rest on the yard below.

More block time came and went. On some occasions I remember being back on the wing and the night clocky screw coming to my cell door and opening the flap and telling me through the slit in the door I was nicked and for the guvnor in the morning. For burning my bedding, I remember him saying. I pointed out my bedding was all correct and on my bunk, but he was having none of it, so I was nicked and taken in front of the number one guvnor the next morning to answer to my fire starting ways. I'd not burnt any sheets or blankets, but it didn't matter. I was found guilty and taken back down the block. Sent down there for an offence I'd not committed, while being in prison for a crime that I shouldn't have been in there for in the first place, was just the piss-take that my life seemed to be back then. I would punch the back of the steel door in frustration until I collapsed, exhausted from the pain in my fists.

The whole prison had got these official white sheets of paper under the doors a few weeks after the minor riots had calmed down. The paper stated that certain attendees of certain courts would not be returning to HMP Moorland and that after their hearing some cons would transfer to a new private run prison in Doncaster with the nickname Doncatraz.

Premiere Prisons was an American-based company that had moved into the private sector of running jails in the UK, and this was its debut. On the letters the Leeds courts and Huddersfield courts were the first to be re-transferred, and then later it was the turn of Bradford. The Wakefield magistrate was the last on the list.

So Moorland gradually became like a ghost prison until our day back at court came. We didn't go to court on the day for the judge-in-chambers hearing, as it was a closed affair where your solicitor went into the judge's office and tried to plead your case for bail. If we got the green light, they would release us from Moorland, but if it was a knock back, then we would leave the next morning on a Group Four van for Doncatraz.

Chapter 7

The wait to hear from the solicitors was stressful. If we didn't get the judge-in-chambers bail, then we would stay on remand, and they had informed us it could take anything up to a year before we got a court date for the crown. So it was a major decision, and one that we prayed went our way.

Around mid-afternoon I got a call to go to the visits room to meet with my solicitor. I knew as soon as I clocked his face it was bad news. I tried to listen and process the positive talk that Mr Batty was waffling on with, but the long shot of it all was, I would now spend at least a year in prison on a rape charge, a crime I never committed.

The next morning after a fitful night's sleep we were put through the reception and placed on the van and we were soon on our way to Doncatraz. We had both heard a few horror stories, via letters, of just what was going on in this new prison. The staff there were not qualified like the old screws and had come through a short training course after leaving normal types of jobs. So you had Bob and Tom, who six weeks ago had worked at a baker or a sales office, trying to control some of the worst violent youth offenders in the country. It was a recipe for disaster, and the cons had taken over the place. What seemed more worrying was that as some areas had gone into the prison before others, they had formed gangs and were running the drugs on certain wings and intimidating other cons who had come later down the line.

It was Sheffield con youths that were the majority in numbers, and by the time we entered as the last court moved, we entered the wing to pure chaos. Add on top of this the charge we were dealing with, we had a fight on our hands from day one. The prison also felt different. It was all high tech and very clinical looking compared to Moorland. You walked down long white corridors and the doors only opened when you looked up at the cameras set into the ceiling. It made a sound like something from *Star Trek* as it whooshed open to let you pass into another part of the corridor.

As the screw turned the key in the only iron gates I had seen, which were the entrances to the wings, we walked into a pure wall of sound. It was like some adult's crazy playground full of human chimps that had gone wild and were out of control. It wasn't just the nature of our charge that brought red-hot irons sailing through the air in front of us or scolding hot mop buckets of water cascading down the stairs. Everyone had received the same mental welcome.

Even under these circumstances, we soon found our feet and settled into life on the wing. It was different in here, as you could come out of your cell and leave it open and sit about in the open area in the middle to play cards or pool or get on the phone or just get a shower. Or if you preferred staying on your bunk in your cell reading, it was your choice to do so. It was a little easier than the twenty-three hour bang up we had endured seven days a week in Moorland.

We had both got into the habit of smoking a lot of weed throughout the day and night and taking any sleeping tablets we could get our hands on. It's not something I like to think of myself as being like now, but right then we both needed anything to take the edge off the seriousness of what we were being put through for nothing. Occasionally I went to the gym, and we went out on exercise every day, weather permitting, but we had both become dependent on getting through the day with the help of drugs.

I wasn't sleeping at all, and I had noticed in the showers one day that my hair was falling out with the stress. I had also lost quite a lot of weight as I was just picking at my food and most of the time living off pot noodles or duffs from the server at teatime.

We both had regular visits, and it was difficult to sit for a few hours with family and to see them get up and go out of one door to freedom and for us to go the other way back to our cells. It was all so surreal and sometimes I just felt like trying to walk right out of the front door with my family. My mind was just so fixed on the fact that I had done nothing wrong and it just seemed unnatural to walk back to a cell when I should have been getting in the car and driving home with my loved ones.

The first few months were the hardest I've ever had to deal with in my entire life. The stress of being incarcerated for something you have not done is overwhelming at times. But to sit and think some people just assumed I was a rapist because I had been remanded was a step too far. I guess this situation can happen to anyone given the right lying circumstances. Yet my case was full of facts that pointed to my obvious innocence. I would ponder for days on end just why the police had believed this bag of lies.

The solicitor's firm didn't seem to do much. I would go on a legal visit to hear that nothing much had changed, and that it was best I waited to speak to the QC appointed to represent me at court. Then, days later, a legal-looking letter would be slid under my door and I would rip it open in apprehension of some progressive news, only to read they were just confirming that they had been up to visit me. I would rip it into little pieces while cursing at the four walls that I was being taken the fuckin' piss out of.

It didn't take long before we were down the block again on suspicion of drug dealing on the wing, and I just didn't care. A cell was a cell in my mind. They could have put me in Alcatraz, and it wouldn't have made the slightest bit of difference to me. In my head, I could only think until I was outside the actual prison walls, then it didn't matter where they kept me. It was a dangerous attitude to hold, and I probably suffered all the more for having it.

The block charges never amounted to anything, and the guvnor would come up each morning to every cell and ask if all was okay. You just said: "yeah" and let him move on. It was all for show and if you had said something was wrong, then nothing would get done, anyway.

I recall on one occasion, after my seven days had run over into something like nineteen, that I'd kicked off and barricaded my door. They just took it off the other way and gave me a bit of a shove about. Another time, I went on hunger strike because they refused me access to the phones for a week. They would leave jam roly-poly duff and hot piping custard just outside the door, and the waft of glorious scents would rumble the old gut. I think I did about ten days until I caved in with a bowl full of golden sponge pudding and custard.

The worst thing that hurt me the most, not physically but mentally, was when I got back on the wing and they brought a hairdresser in to cut our hair. I had put my name down on the list, but when my turn came I felt so awkward being sat there with this young woman. The stigma of my charge had ruined my confidence and I just remember sitting there hoping to God she didn't ask me what I was in for.

Not that it makes the incident stand out. But as I'd finished and gone back to my wing, this kid who I'd not seen before was hovering around the gate area nosing in. I didn't think much about it, and the hairdresser told the screw near the gate she was going on a break. The guard opened the gate and escorted her back down the corridor. As they were out of site, this kid who was still hovering about outside the gate called me over.

I approached carefully, but not really thinking, and before I knew it this sly little wanker had whipped a plastic mug, for drinking tea, from behind his back and launched it at me. My reactions were fast, but not fast enough and my mind in that instant got ready to feel the hot sugary burn that many uses as a weapon in the nick. I wish it had been hot water or tea, as the familiar stench of piss wafted up my nose. He accompanied this assault with a barrage of abuse, calling me a rapist cunt. He then disappeared back to the end of the landing out of sight while I tried my best to break through the metal gate to kill him.

Looking back, I'm glad that I didn't possess the strength then to pull that gate open, because I snapped at that point and I would have killed the fucker with my bare hands if I'd got a hold of him.

I washed in the shower and it was the first time my eyes welled up with tears at just what was happening to me. I washed the pain away and composed myself and got some fresh clobber on and tried to laugh it off. But it still makes me livid even twenty-five years later. To be judged like that when I was innocent, was just so devastating.

Chapter 8

In our cell, the Rat was now using heroin. He was knocking about with a few junky fuckers from the Sheffield area, and it had gone from him finding an empty cell throughout the day for a little toot with them, to him bringing some smack into our cell and chasing the dreaded dragon throughout the evening. I continued smoking my weed and doing bongs, which I fashioned out of plastic Coca-Cola bottles. It didn't take long for him to get himself a little habit, but he wasn't that hooked. I worried though, because at that point, and for many years later, I felt we were in this bind together. If only he had blurted out his secret back then!

To be honest, we were both lost into the system and it felt like we just didn't care what happened anymore. In the back of my mind I knew that once it got to Crown Court and they heard all the evidence, then even a chimpanzee could see we were not lying and they would give us not guilty verdicts and set us free. I had looked over what paperwork I possessed a few times but wasn't really bothered thinking about the trial too much because it seemed so far away at that stage.

At one point I thought I had seen a way to break through the wing roof and get up on to the outside prison roof. It wasn't to escape, but just to get the message out to the media about what was happening to us. For weeks I planned it, building things up for what I would need like food and water and materials for making my point visual to the media when the time came to climb and break through. A few days before I was about to get ready to do it, late into the night, the cell door burst open and this screw just punched me full force in the mouth as I woke from the disturbance. I remember fighting with him until they all ganged up like they do and dragged me outside and twisted me up into the stress positions they teach them, and moved me off bent up double with both my arms up my back and my wrists at snapping point.

When I entered the block wing, the whole place was going nuts with noise. The block, which was full of adult prisoners as the prison was half and half, was on my case as the screws had already tipped off a few of the older cons about our charge. They dragged me onto the circular block to a mass of shouting and chants of,

"Hang em hang em hang em hang em hang em hang em hang em!"

To kind of give you an example of just how much I had lost it and how much I just didn't give a shit about all these strangers and their opinions, I could not give a fuck at the drop of a hat back then. I had been getting stamped address envelopes sent into the prison. The reason I had been getting these was because the screws were ripping the stamps off our mail as people were hiding things under them. But legally, they couldn't touch your incoming mail that had self-addressed envelopes included in your original letter. Underneath my stamps were old style sheet acid tabs.

The screws when they had ripped me out of bed and dragged me down to the block had been so busy trying to break my wrists they had not given me a search. So after about ten minutes of them leaving me alone in my empty block cell with the chant of "hang him hang him" electric in the air, I dropped one of my tabs and sat with my back to the steel door and zoned out. The trip was deep and long and strange under the circumstances. The muppets shouting at me soon got bored, and I tripped out into a free world for a while.

When I eventually got back up on the wing and settled back as best I could into the monotonous life I had there, a strange thing happened that should have given me a clue to the Rat's secret. It was one afternoon when the screws walked into the wing main area and shouted the RAT over and said he had a visit. Now, it wasn't proper family and friends visiting time, so he had asked in front of me who it was, and the screw had said it was some detectives from Wakefield who wanted to speak to him. He looked at me a little alarmed and disappeared out the gate to take the visit. When he returned I was sat on the bottom tier of our bunk beds in our pad reading a book on the life of Oscar Wilde, which included 'The Ballad of Reading Gaol'. When he got back in and sat down, I asked him what the visit had been all about to which he replied,

"They're just fishing mate, trying to clear up some unsolved fuckin' cases and trying to fit me up some more."

As I've stated at this point in my life, I felt we were in this together and it outraged me at hearing that the pigs were trying to give him even more shit.

He said, "They're looking into old cases of rape and asking me all types of questions and showing me photo fits of faces who they think are responsible."

Now, I was never at this visit and I couldn't say at all what actually happened, but the Rat laughed it all off to me saying they were asking him about a rape where the suspect wore cowboy boots! Which knowing the Rat's preference for designer clobber didn't fit one bit. I kind of just put the incident out of my mind. A few more months of monotony went by in the same old routine of remand prison life. But I wondered why, if they were looking into old rape cases, the police didn't want to speak to me as well. We were both co-accused of this charge, so why not ask me? There must have been a reason they focused on the Rat.

It was also a time I remember very well on a positive note for the case. One that I didn't see coming at all. I had received a letter from a lad called Charlie, who was an old pal, and a cousin of this lying tart that had put me on remand. He is dead now of a suicide, God bless him, but back then he had written to me asking how we were and saying how sorry he was and that he didn't believe it for one minute. The letter was appreciated, but what was telling was he left a mobile phone number at the end of his letter asking me to call it ASAP because it was

MISS LEGALLY ANONYMOUS'S dad's number and he wanted to speak to me to help with our case.

(Perfected Grounds of Appeal by Judge Rodney Jameson)

<u>**Judges Reaction and Summing up**</u>

Judge refused to allow evidence from MISS LEGALLY ANONYMOUS'S father that she was herself the product of a "one-night stand" whom he had rejected and never seen. He ruled it was "irrelevant". This view coloured the whole of his approach to the defence case.

Chapter 9

I got **MISS LEGALLY ANONYMOUS'S** dad on the phone willing to go to our solicitor and write a statement in our favour saying she was a product of a one night stand and that she hated men and that she was a compulsive liar. He actually wrote this statement which the old bastard Hutchinson ruled irrelevant to the case!

Her own dad saying she was a compulsive liar yet in the judge's opinion, he wouldn't allow it into the trial as it was irrelevant to a case about who's lying! Again the ludicrousness of this still hurts my brain all these decades later. Before the judge ruled it irrelevant to the case, it had become a piece of evidence crucial to our innocence and it had been a major mood booster inside the four walls of the ever shrinking cell. I felt confident that with this evidence and the obvious points that didn't add up in her statement compared to ours, that we had a good chance of it getting kicked out of court before the trial even got anywhere near under way.

How wrong could I have been! About a month later, we had both been down the block again, charged with suspicion of assault. A lad from Leeds had taken a beating in a cell one afternoon. He was looking like the elephant man and they had taken him all wrapped up in a hoody up to the showers that were quiet and told to wash himself up as best he could. I don't think he grassed, but the screws couldn't help but notice his head wounds, and so the screws had dragged us down the block again on suspicion of being involved.

They had stripped us bare this time, and we both sat in cells side by side, stark bollock naked. Soon, with the help of a few lads, we got ourselves dressed in some shorts from the gym and sweatshirts. I remember the block screws doing their rounds and looking through our cell door flaps to gloat at our naked vulnerability. They were so mad when they realised we had managed to get some clothes on, like some magic trick.

They came in with the baton team the next time, ripping at our new bits of clothing. We were told, once naked and back behind closed doors, that we would be getting moved first thing in the morning out of Yorkshire! Now this was bullshit because you had to be housed in your nearest local remand centre. But they tried using all our block charges against us, even though most times, there was no evidence to support the charges.

Early in the morning, they came thundering into my pad and walked me off the block wing down towards reception. I kept on telling them that wherever they thought they were sending me; I wouldn't be going and that I would be having my tea in Doncatraz! They just laughed at me and said that I was being moved to Leicester. It wasn't sounding good, and we both decided once the Rat had joined me in the reception holding cell to barricade in the best we could. We pulled on some benches and trapped them up against the door and wedged ourselves behind that with our feet up against the wall. It was a solid barrier, and they failed to barge it open. The holding cell from waist height up, was all glass. The screws were furious and all starting to congregate around the glass mouthing words of violence and what they were going to do to us both once they got their hands on us. We were determined that we weren't going anywhere. We had been told by this old timer that if the van didn't get us into Leicester prison by a certain time; I think it was four p.m., then they couldn't accept you or something like that. So we tried our best to delay this illegal move.

Once, they had brought the principal officer to the glass windows, and we had told him we were going fuckin' nowhere. He sulked off, and they left us for a good half hour, wondering what their next move was going to be. When this giant looking screw gave the door one last boot and shove, which we only just held back, they changed tactics. I heard the industrial size drill's noise before I saw it. They were now outside the plated glass front, steadily unscrewing the bolts on each windowpane. As they were doing this, the one with the drill was grinning like a maniac while his screw buddies behind him were slavering at the mouth with anticipation of getting their hands on us. Just as they were about to remove the first pane of plexiglass, we opened up the door and walked out.

They went a bit nuts pushing and dragging us about. They put us into search rooms and gave us a strip search. I'd broken both big toes playing football against the screws team a week earlier and had both toes bandaged up. They pulled the bandages off roughly, while I protested that the nurse had bandaged them up and they wouldn't find anything in there. They found jack shit, and then they put me onto this Group Four van, destination Tiger Road. Before I boarded the van, they had made me run a gauntlet of angry screws who had lined up all along the entrance to the doorway where I needed to step out to board. Six of them on each side delivered a few digs to the head and body on my way through! With one of them giving me a real boot to the ribs as I hurried past the best I could.

When the Rat and a few other cons were loaded up, four of us altogether, we drove off out of Doncatraz's foreboding gates heading south. The clock was ticking, and all four of us had the same motivation to get the move scuppered. There were two Group Four screws on board. One driving and one in the back where we were all locked in our sweaty, plastic cubicles. They communicated via radio because the van was in transit.

Half an hour into the journey, this Asian lad in the back started screaming and shouting, saying he was feeling suicidal and that he was claustrophobic. The screw in the back told him to shut the fuck up, while radioing through to the driver to tell him what all the racket was about and that he was okay, and everything was under control. Ten minutes after the first incident in the back, I heard the screw in a panicked voice pass my cubicle screaming into the radio for the driver to hurry to the nearest place he could safely pull over. The next thing I remember was shooting face first into the plastic wall in front of me as the driver screeched to a halt on some hard shoulder.

The lad in the back had somehow hung himself with his shoelace. I heard the screw from the back talking franticly to the driver, who was now in the back of the van to help. There was an urgent discussion between them, and then the driver ran back out and got the van running again and we sped off. I can't recall where abouts we were when this happened, but we eventually pulled into some local hospital's A&E ambulance bay. The screws got nurses with stretchers outside and took the lad away. It was all a blag to kill time and get the van turned around back to Donny.

A good hour we waited in the back to see if we were going to get turned back right there and then because of this lad, but our hope soon turned to despair because we heard the Group Four screw climb back on board, and then the next minute these doctors and nurses accompanying the lad came back to the van with the other screw. We were soon back to four again in the back with the two screws radioing Doncatraz telling them about the delay and that they were full steam ahead now to HMP Tiger Road, Leicester.

Half an hour down the motorway the Rat chocked himself that bad that he burst all the blood vessels in his eyes and we spun around again on the way back to the same hospital, with the screw in the back going mental to the driver in the front on his radio. As his stretcher appeared, flying out to meet us as we pulled into the same parking space we had left only an hour ago, the Rat gave me a wink as he lay back on the stretcher.

I don't know what he did in there, but we were waiting hours, and when he boarded the Group Four van again, the screw in the back got on his radio to the prison at Leicester and I heard him say that with all the delays and the distance left to drive still, that he didn't think they would arrive in time for the prisoners to be processed.

We all cheered in the back and he shouted at us in frustration for us to shut the hell up. He radioed through to the driver and told him he needed to head back towards Doncatraz. As the van left the hospital, the driver with all the confusion made a wrong turn out of the grounds and he had to stop and do a U-turn. We cheered the loudest when he put the van's back wheels into this ditch as he did the U-turn and almost got it stuck. A few minutes of revving and we were back on the road and heading the right way.

The faces of the reception screws at Doncatraz were a picture. They were mad as hell that we were back, and we didn't stop the wind up, shouting to any screw we noticed that "We told you we would be back."

I was back down the block by evening time and sat back in the cell they had pulled me out of that same morning. It felt like a small victory against the system.

Chapter 10

I had more or less lost the concept of time at this stage. Every day was just the same old monotonous repeat. I think about ten months into the remand we finally got our date for trial at Leeds Crown Court. I recall us both trying hard for a few weeks to clean up our acts, referring to the drugs we were using to cope. The Rat reduced his intake of heroin and smoked more skunk, while I knocked the trippy bongs on the head and settled for a good few long rolled spliffs to put me out like a light at bedtime.

When we got down to seriously looking over the large files of white paper, I recall us being even more astonished at how ridiculous it all sounded. What she had said in her statements sounded very 'police' written. She had made three different statements, and each one contradicted the other in ways that screamed out that she was making all this up!

It's weird when you're reading a statement and you're disgusted with how outrageous the crime sounds being spoken about, yet you then get such a sickening sensation when you realise the reality of it all and that they are talking about you. It was unbelievable. Something that stuck out to me was, one morning we were both sat on the bottom bunk in our cell reading the paperwork for trial, when the Rat read something that made him angry. In my statement to the police from the initial arrest, I had mentioned him cutting his penis. Again, without knowing the Rat's secret, I didn't at that time understand why he was so pissed off that I had mentioned it! Twenty-five years later, I know now why the wanker had got a sweat on and why he was annoyed that I had mentioned that.

I had witnessed a few things that didn't make sense about how he was acting, but in those circumstances at that moment in time, I had no clue and just let them slide. I had the firm attitude that it was us against the system, and I didn't think the reason I might be so deep in the shit was so close to me all the while. A few more incidents happened on the wing, with fights and nicking's and the usual rubbish that accompanies prison life. It was all irrelevant though, as the trial loomed large in the background of my mind and it was fast approaching the day when we got the chance to take the stand and give our opinions on this disgrace of an arrest and remand. I was looking forward to getting a not guilty and going home after what was to be thirteen months of hard remand time before our day in court.

By this time I was suffering from hallucinogenic stress. Under the intensity of the situation, I was seeing things that were not real and having serious nightmares that upon waking had me in a real panic. The weed and acid had not helped, yet it felt more like the stress that was giving me the trip out of late. But I muddled on the best I could, getting long cold showers, trying to wake my brain up from this long remand sleep.

I can't even remember the night before the trial in our cell, but I assume we got an early night and tried to be fresh for court. They had brought us in our best clothes from the outside, to make a good impression on the judge and jury, and ironed them ready and had shaved and tried our best to get ready for whatever the next five days would bring. They had allocated five days for the trial at Leeds to go over all the evidence and hear from the witnesses that they would bring up into the witness box to speak either against us or for us.

Some wanker screws from the reception at Doncatraz said as a parting gift before they placed us in the Group Four van, that they would see us later that evening. We just ignored these shallow minded petty folks and got on the van to drive to Leeds. I remember seeing how busy the traffic was in the centre of Leeds as the van turned through the back roads of the town hall and pulled up into the back street where the entrance was located for the combined courts. They processed us through and handed us over to the Leeds court screws and placed us downstairs in the cells to wait until they called us up to the courtroom.

It was a familiar space to me as I had sat in the same cell a few years back when I had been sent down for robberies. Yet this was so different, it had such an intense feeling when our QC's came down to speak to us individually. Tim Stead for the Rat who is now Judge Stead, and QC Rodney Mellor Maples Jameson for me, who is now Judge Jameson at the very same court. So, when you read later in this story about my perfected grounds of appeal by Rodney, they are the thoughts of a Crown Court judge now.

Around nine a.m. they opened us up and told us to follow the guards up the stairs, which led to the courtroom. Upon entering the court, it again seemed all so surreal. The judge wasn't sat on his throne yet.

Just the clerks and assistants busily moving around, getting everything ready for when Judge Arthur Hutchinson made his grand entrance. I knew nothing of the judge back then, but all these years later I can give you some understanding of the man who was about to ruin my life by siding with an obvious liar.

He was born in Huddersfield yet lived in Ilkley, West Yorkshire. He was the son of the late Ted Hutchinson, a noted Huddersfield Solicitor. Educated at Silcoates Private School, which is just up the hill from the village of Wrenthorpe where I live now, and then studied law at Emmanuel College, Cambridge. But his university studies came only after a spell in the army and a brush with death. Hutchinson received a commission, at age nineteen, into the Northumberland Fusiliers and served in Kenya where British troops faced a rebellion by the Mau Mau. A tribesman using a bow and arrow shot at Second-Lieutenant Hutchinson, but the arrow missed his throat by a fraction of an inch. Which in my opinion was a real shame?

He was called to the Middle Temple Bar in 1958 and became a barrister. In 1979 he was appointed a QC and was a highly respected Crown Court judge for many years.

So, in all honesty I can only assume that when he came out of his chambers and took his seat in front of me in 1994, senior detectives had already advised him he was to push for a guilty verdict at all costs. Now, please don't tell me this sort of corruption does not go on. Who knows what gets said in chambers and what gets passed along to ears that decide our fates?

69

We were told to all rise as he entered. He then looked at us both like shit upon his shoe and sat down, thinking he looked all regal in his large robe and wig.

They looked ridiculous in their silly outfits to me, and I had to hold back right from the off, because I wanted to shout at him about my treatment so far on remand and demand he immediately set me free from this joke of a charge. But I kept schtum and like an idiot put my faith into the mighty hands of the British law system. I had committed no offence. You get found not guilty. You go home. Simple.

Oh, how I wish I'd had that tribesman's bow and arrow to fire my own shot. Maybe it would have woken the stupid old bastard up, because throughout this trial he was asleep for major parts of it.

Chapter 11

The first day was very much swallowed up by formalities in getting the case moving. We had both got excellent support in the public gallery, with our families and friends looking over as we stood in the court, giving us the thumbs up and smiles of encouragement. They all knew we had suffered on remand and them, just like us, hoped that any day soon this nightmare would end, and we would accompany them home. Like I've stated, the first day was a bit of a non-event in the courtroom, but for me the stress was about to get ramped up to the max.

The court adjourned for the day around four p.m. and they took us back down to the cells to wait for the van to drive us back to HMP Doncatraz. About twenty minutes later, I heard a van back into the alley outside the row of cells. The Rat was in the cell next door to me, and I heard the gate swing open and a guard shout over to the Leeds court screws,

"Have you got FP0471 ?"

I then heard his cell door being opened, and him being led out to be secured in the van. So, I'm waiting for them to come back to get me out and put me in the van too. But after about ten minutes, my door had still not opened. Then the next thing I heard was the Group Four van engine erupt into life and drive away!

I'm stood at my cell door shouting out into the corridor, trying to get one of the Leeds court screws to notice, thinking they have made a mistake and they will have to bring the van back sharpish. Five minutes later the steel flap on my cell door gets lowered and two screws, whose faces I didn't recognise from the day's proceedings, leaned in towards my face and I could see they had in their hands some paperwork. The oldest of the two then shocked me with what he said.

"You're not going on that van to Donny mate!"

To which I replied that I should be as that's where I had travelled from this very morning and that all my belongings were at Doncatraz. They both just laughed at me through the flap and said,

"Nice try, but we have sussed you out!"

I played dumb while my mind was spinning, trying to figure out what was going on. The older one again piped up and said,

"You're twenty-one and you have been lying about your age, the Armley van is what you're going on!"

My head was spinning at this news, but I knew they were right. When I'd turned twenty-one months earlier I'd blagged my paperwork in Doncaster when they had admitted us into their custody. I'd even had my friends and family send me happy twenty today badges on cards to keep the blag going because I had not wanted to be separated from my co-accused, and

I'd certainly not fancied going into the adult system alone with this charge hanging over me.

It was a bad day though to get sussed out, as I now wondered just what the hell would be in store for me as I headed into adult prison for the first time. As a northerner, I had heard about the house on the hill. HMP Armley was originally known as Leeds Borough Gaol and completed in 1847. It had been a site for execution by hanging from 1847–1961. It was a grim and forbidding prison in line with the Victorian ideas of reform. They had only stopped hanging people behind its walls thirty-four years before I was on my way in with a charge that, before the abolishment of the death penalty, would have been a hangable offence. It's reputably, one of the most haunted buildings in West Yorkshire.

I waited in the cell for another twenty minutes and then the cell door flew open and the two Armley screws called me forward and checked my details against this clipboard they were holding. The next thing I was in the van and heading through the Leeds traffic towards the house on the hill. I was getting worried now and feeling nervous. Any move is quite daunting, but to be starred up to the big-con jail from a youth prisoner is always a big deal. To do it on the first day of a major trial is just nuts.

As the van turned onto the roundabout that takes you towards HMP Armley, I noticed it through the van window, high and forbidding up on its high hill at the top of Gloucester Terrace. It's like some old haunted-looking dark castle perched up there. Before long I was outside its enormous gates and the van was radioing through to be admitted. My nerves were in bits at this moment, but I just knew I had to hold it together or I would be in serious trouble inside here.

After they had processed me through the desk area, one of the more decent old time screws on reception put me into a holding cell not as packed with other cons arriving back from court. No one in my cell asked me who I was or what I was in for, which suited me fine right then. So, when they finally moved us onto the wing and put us into another large holding pen, someone finally got around to focusing on me.

"What ya in for mate?"

Now I knew that at this point I was in danger of getting jumped. There were around twenty cons in this cell. But I felt I had to play it straight and that the best policy was to just explain how I was getting stitched up, so I replied,

"Rape mate, total fuckin' stitch up!"

Luckily, they were a decent bunch and could see I was new to the adult system and that I was a decent lad really, so they just wished me luck with the trial, which I had said I was going not guilty and that there was zero evidence against me. The screws came and moved me to a single cell, and I got the first night out of the way in the house on the hill.

Chapter 12

They unlocked me and moved me back to reception the next morning ready for court. My clothes were all creased, and I had no toiletries to get ready with, so I'd not been able to shave, and worst of all I had not been back to my old cell at Doncatraz, where all my legal paperwork was. So it was a disaster as far as anyone could see for the start of a major trial.

Once I had arrived back at Leeds Crown Court, I got to see the Rat who was shocked that I had not arrived back at Doncaster with him. He had thought I was in the van until they had gone through the reception. We had a brief chat about my adventure to Armley and an hour later, after being locked in the court dungeon cells, the door opened and in strode my QC, Rodney. He himself was not aware of my adventure, and I told him I wasn't going up into the court until I received some decent toiletries to shave and do my hair and brush my teeth.

He said he would address this to the judge. We were called up promptly at nine a.m. and I was given twenty minutes to go back down to the cell area to sort out my ragged appearance. My mother had nipped out to a local shop nearby and bought me the things I needed to tidy myself up a bit for the start of the second day of trial. Proceedings got under way at 9.30 a.m.

It was the prosecution's opening today, with a few witnesses brought in to give their evidence against us and the lead witness **MISS LEGALLY**

ANONYMOUS'S chance to take the stand and blurt out her lies.

When she entered the courtroom, I couldn't believe my eyes. When I had last seen her, she was a hippy looking girl with long blonde dreaded or braided hair. I hardly recognised her as she walked into the Crown Courtroom. She had on a black business suit and she'd had her hair cut into a bob style and straightened. She didn't have the caked on makeup either. It was at this point that I really started to worry, and the thoughts racing through my mind were ones that she had definitely come to hoodwink the judge and jury and get us sent down for a crime she had made up. If anyone was about to be guilty of a crime, it was her. She was about to commit perjury on the Crown Court stand.

Here's a brief insight into this poor rape victim's mind-set as she entered court that morning. Obviously, I was told this later from my mother, as I couldn't see what was occurring outside the courtroom doors. At Crown Court, on the day of the trial, my mum, and her friend Elaine and some of my friends had been outside the courtroom, all sat on the right-hand side. My mum recalls that **MISS LEGALLY ANONYMOUS'S** friends sat opposite, on the left. When **MISS LEGALLY ANONYMOUS** entered the court waiting room, she didn't know my mum or friends, and didn't look towards the right. My mum said as soon as she came through the door, she looked at her scruffy mates and did a pantomime like curtsey and shouted,

"Hiya, star of the shows here!"

So the farce of a trial started, and she gave her evidence that second morning, and it was astonishing the blatant lies and contradictions that came out of her mouth. Her lies were just so goddamn blatant that it was hard to see why the trial wasn't being stopped for perjury right there on the spot. Good old Judge Arthur Hutchinson even gave her a ten-minute recess at one point, because she had got into a serious case of perjury when one of her prosecution witnesses, who she had called to the stand, made her out to be lying through her teeth. Now I have to point out here that these were her witnesses, they were there to back up her bullshit lies! What they did was to make it crystal clear to everyone present in the courtroom she was one hundred per cent lying through her teeth. She realised this while she stood on the stand and burst into tears. It was like some poor play from where I was standing looking at this farce play out in front of me. Good Old Arthur, the judge even leant forward and offered her some tissues he had in a box in front of his bench. It was incredible, and she disappeared out of the courtroom double doors with this chaperone, there to help her from the witness protection team, or some copper assigned to help her through her ordeal!

I have heard from reliable witnesses who sat outside the courtroom in the waiting area where **MISS LEGALLY ANONYMOUS** went to compose herself, that she spoke to people who had not even gone into court yet who were there to give evidence under oath. Even that detective Mc DX was hovering about, and I will mention a little later just how corrupt he was out there chatting to defence witnesses, who were there to prove we were both speaking the truth.

At this point from my limited knowledge of the law system, I expected the trial to stop right there and then. I know now, with a much broader knowledge, that the case should have been stopped. There are just so many areas of law where this joke of a trial should have ended, and my body and mind set free from the chains of lies that had encircled me.

I won't try to go through the trial in exact order, as it's hard to recall, and I don't want to write this out as if it were some court document to follow. I have included in the book legal paperwork directly transcribed from the original perfected grounds of appeal etc that the now Judge Jameson prepared for me, as they show in proper order the major discrepancies throughout the whole trial and summing up by Judge Hutchinson.

As I recall how the trial made me feel then, it was like the jury thawed towards me in my mind on the second day, especially after hearing some blatant contradictions in the morning regarding **MISS LEGALLY ANONYMOUS'S** last statement, and some witnesses, she and the police had to take the stand for her. Early things that stood out for me, and which should have stood out a mile for the twelve jury members, was the evidence of **MISS LEGALLY ANONYMOUS'S** neighbour. She gave a statement to the police stating that she was a light sleeper and her bedroom was on the adjoining wall of **MISS LEGALLY ANONYMOUS'S** own bedroom and that regularly she had been woken up at all hours by disturbances coming from **MISS LEGALLY ANONYMOUS'S** bedroom. Now, on the night in question, she slept soundly and didn't hear a thing, which when the defence in the courtroom pointed out to **MISS LEGALLY ANONYMOUS,** on the stand, that in her statement she stated she was screaming out in pain and shouting for us to stop. Judge Hutchinson in his wisdom pointed out to the jury that maybe the witness, who even though she had given a statement, didn't want to attend the trial. The judge made it clear to the jury she was 'clearly keeping her head down!' What the hell does that even mean or have to do with the obviousness of the contradiction just made. He seemed to do this throughout the whole trial and never once defined points we had proved to the jury. He had a clear bias against us from the start and even Judge Jameson, who was then my QC, said so in his comments in my perfected grounds of appeal.

I supposed the question that could get asked was this, why didn't the neighbour hear us having sex? As I've stated, **MISS LEGALLY ANONYMOUS** was moaning and enjoying the sex, but it wasn't a loud moaning. She moaned with pleasure though throughout the entire night. I guess the answer is simple, there is a massive difference between someone moaning softly, and someone getting brutally raped and screaming out in pain and shouting for us to stop!

(Perfected Grounds of Appeal by Judge Rodney Jameson)

(FROM NEIGHBOURS STATEMENT

Complainants account of brutal rape,5 or 6 times by 2 men over the course of 2hours during which she screamed in pain and at the appellant and the RAT, contradicted by)

(a) EVIDENCE OF MISS GREY, THE COMPLAINANTS NEXT DOOR NEIGHBOUR (IN A PAIR OF SEMI DETATCHED HOUSES) THAT SHE WAS A LIGHT SLEEPER, OFTEN DISTURBED BY NOISE FROM THE COMPLAINANTS HOUSE, WHO SLEPT ON THE OTHER SIDE OF THE WALL FROM THE SCENE OF INTERCOURSE ON THE NIGHT IN QUESTION, UNDISTURBED.

Chapter 13

Here's another piece of her evidence that makes no sense at all. It makes little sense because she is lying about being raped and I have suffered a serious miscarriage of justice. She contradicted her statement when under cross-examination on the stand. She said the reason the neighbour didn't hear anything was because she didn't make much attempt at stopping us from raping her because we had a CS gas canister in her face throughout the entire ordeal. I must point out here too, before I get back into the cross-examination part, that she made three statements and only in her final one did she mention this gas threat. The cross-examiner tripped her up on the stand, by getting her to reveal that she only recalled seeing the gas after the attack, and that it was downstairs on top of the TV!

Again, how the trial wasn't stopped right there, I will never know. She's saying in her statement that we held the CS gas in front of her face, yet on the stand she only remembers seeing the gas downstairs on the TV. Also in the same vein, she says she's screaming out in pain and shouting out. Which is it?

PERFECTED GROUNDS OF APPEAL STATING WHEN WE WERE SEPARATELY ARRESTED WITHOUT ANY WARNING, NO CS GAS WAS FOUND IN EITHER PROPERTY OR ON US ETC...}

NO CAN OF C.S. GAS WAS FOUND IN HER HOUSE. NO SUCH CAN WAS SEEN BY THE

POLICE OFFICER WHO SPOKE TO HYDE AND THE RAT AT 4.30 AM. NO SUCH CAN WAS FOUND AT EITHER DEFENDANT'S HOME WHEN THEY WERE ARRESTED WITHOUT WARNING. BOTH DENIED ITS EXISTENCE.

MISS LEGALLY ANNOYMOUS DID NOT MENTION C.S GAS TO THE FIRST TWO PEOPLE SHE SPOKE WITH AFTER THE ALLEGED ATTACK. BOTH SEPARATE CONVERSATIONS WITH TWO DIFFERENT FEMALES, THE SECOND OF THESE FEMALES GIVEN A DETAILED ACCOUNT FROM MISS LEGALLY ANNONYMOUS.
BY THE DATE OF HER FIRST STATEMENT TO THE POLICE, THERE IS NOW REFRENCE TO C.S. GAS. HOWEVER, CONTRARY TO HER REPEATED ASSERTION IN EVIDENCE THAT THE ENTIRE RAPE (WHICH OCCURRED UPSTAIRS) WAS AT THE NOZZLE OF THE CAN, THE STATEMENT INDICATES THAT SHE WAS NOT AWARE OF THE CAN BEING UPSTAIRS UNTIL INTERCOURSE WAS OVER.

SUMMING UP
THE JUDGE DEALT WITH PHOTOGRAPH 10 (A PHOTO OF HER BEDROOM FLOOR) BY INVITING THE JURY TO CONCLUDE THAT MISS LEGALLY ANNONYMOUS MAY HAVE IN FACT BEEN THREATENED WITH THE CAN IN PHOTOGRAPH 10, WHICH SHE MAY HAVE BELIEVED WAS A C.S. GAS CAN. THE JUDGE SUGGESTED IT WAS A LAGER CAN THE DEFENDENTS HAD BROUGHT WITH

THEM. IN FACT IT IS A DEODORANT/HAIRSPRAY MADE BY KARL LAGERFELD. WHICH CLEARLY BELONGS TO MISS LEGALY ANNONYMOUS, AND WHICH SHE COULD HARDLY HAVE FAILED TO RECOGNIZE

I will tell you which it is. It's the one where a loose women is enjoying having sex with two men, and the next day regrets it and doesn't know how to face her boyfriend who she recently broke up with. That's the proper answer, because nothing in court made any sense, and they say you have to be found guilty beyond any reasonable doubt. It's a fuckin' joke. Because of this, it has ruined my life in so many ways, and I want justice. Proper justice, not some bullshit acquittal. I want compensating and apologising to by all who knew the Rat's secret. Because again, without that important Rat fact in the equation, I don't see how this could happen.

Again, if I rewind just a little into the second day's evidence, heard in court, it can only astound me as to the blatant contradictions given by the prosecution's witnesses on the stand against the so-called victim **MISS LEGALLY ANONYMOUS's** statement. She says she had arrived home on the night in question and falsely claimed we raped her. In her statement she said that when she had returned home, driven by two mates, she had unlocked her front door and they had all entered the house. She, upon discovering me and the Rat sitting in the lounge, had been mad as hell.

What I wasn't aware of until I heard her contradict herself on the stand from what she had said in her statement, was that before she arrived home, she had gone to her ex boyfriends to try get back together with him. Here is what he had to say when questioned about her visit.

PERFECTED GROUNDS OF APPEAL BY JUDGE RODNEY JAMESON
SHE DECIDED TO GO VISIT A MAN NAMED MR GREY. GREY, CALLED BY THE PROSECUTION, SAID THAT HE WAS NOT EXPECTING HER TO VISIT HIS PARENTS HOUSE, AND THAT HER PURPOSE WAS TO FURTHER A RELATIONSHIP WITH HIM. HE HAD SEXUAL INTERCOURSE WITH HER BUT DID NOT REGARD HER AS A GIRLFRIEND. WHEN HE TOLD HER THIS SHE WAS UPSET. SHE WENT HOME TO FIND THE TWO DEFENDENTS IN HER HOUSE, WAITING FOR HER. THE DEFENCE CASE WAS THAT SHE AGREED TO SEXUAL INTERCOURSE WHILST "ON THE REBOUND" AND THAT HER LATER DISTRESS AND COMPLAINTS WERE DUE TO HER REGRETTING THAT.

HER FIRST REPORT THE NEXT MORNING TO A WOMEN AT THE COUNCIL OFFICE WAS THAT A MAN HAD RAPED HER WHILE ANOTHER HELD HER DOWN!

THE WITNESS EVIDENCE WAS AS FOLLOWS.

MISS GREEN. AT 9.30AM 6TH JUNE MISS LEGALLY ANONYMOUS UPSET.

IT WAS SOMETHING SEXUAL. I (GREEN) SUGGESTED IT WAS RAPE. SHE AGREED. NO DETAILS GIVEN. DETAILS BEGAN AT LUNCHTIME.

MISS BROWN. AT 11AM 6TH JUNE. MISS LEGALLY ANONYMOUS SAID, "ONE OF THE MEN HELD HER DOWN WHILST THE OTHER ONE HAD FORCED HIMSELF UPON HER".

"SHE FELT THREATENED BY THEM" THIS IS A VERY DIFFERENT ACCOUNT TO THAT WHICH EMERGED IN HER STATEMENT ON 8TH JUNE. THERE IS EQUALLY NO REFERENCE TO C.S. GAS,

When her prosecution witness and friend gave her statement, she contradicted what **MISS LEGALLY ANONYMOUS** had lied about. What her friend said was that when they arrived in the hallway, **MISS LEGALLY ANONYMOUS** had opened the lounge door and found us sitting there, her friend said that she was embarrassed and when asked if everything was okay, **MISS LEGALLY ANONYMOUS** had said that it was, and that we were her friends. This witness stated that when she had asked **MISS LEGALLY ANONYMOUS** a second time if she was sure she was okay, she had said to her friend she was fine and then kind of showed her friend the door.

Now again, this doesn't add up. You come home to find two strange men in your front room lounge! It's late at night! Luckily, two mates accompany you onto your property. What would you do? It's so obvious that you would have wanted help from those two friends. That you would want them to call the police! Between the three of them they would have got out of the house and looked for help! Yet none of these things happened. **MISS LEGALLY ANONYMOUS** said in her statement she was mad as hell and shouted at us. Her mates said that she was embarrassed yet introduced us as her friends. Another major thing to point out relating to this part was where she had denied ever meeting me before. Well, how did I know where to go to be at her house?

I knew because I had been there around three weeks earlier when I had slept with her that time. She denied this meeting. So again, does that make us two total strangers in her lounge when she got back? If that were the case, they would have called the police. Like her friend who was at the house stated in her statement, that she was shown the door by **MISS LEGALLY ANONYMOUS** who couldn't wait to be alone with the pair of us. It's what she had intended to happen when she had put the offer to us in Bitz Nightclub. The same as when she had laughed and said, "oh you got in through the window I see." Yeah we had, as she had suggested it in the first place, the same way the lad in the Wakey Magistrate's cells had got in.

Chapter 14

The next stand out moment in the Crown Courtroom was when **MISS LEGALLY ANONYMOUS** was led through her statement by her prosecution barrister regarding the injuries she claimed to have received in this brutal attack! It was so hard to stand there as the accused and listen to all this. It sounded horrific, and I can only imagine how the jury felt about us upon hearing about the brutality. I can also imagine the jury wondering just what the hell was going on when they heard the evidence of the police surgeon or doctor who had examined her and who then reported that there were *no internal signs* whatsoever of this brutal and prolonged attack. Also, the amount of injuries she should have suffered according to her detailed statement where she said I was the one who had hurt her, beaten her, kicked her, wrapped my legs around her neck in a choke hold, dug my feet into her back, and slapped her, were not evident. It was a list that I'm sure a woman would receive at least some kind of injury from a grown man who's raping her and being brutal. *No evidence of any kind of injury was reported by the police doctor who they had called to check her over!* Nothing, zilch. Again a bloody joke in the court proceedings and again a point where I feel the trial should have been stopped and both of us set free. But no, they carried on, glossing over these glaring facts. There was nothing, bar a fading bruise, which she said had occurred as part of her brutal beating! They also proved this to be weeks old and fading and nothing at all related on a timescale to the night in question.

{PERFECTED GROUNDS OF APPEAL BY JUDGE JAMESON SHOWING NO INJURIES AT ALL!}

DALE BEGAN THRUSTING HIS PENIS IN REALLY HARD. I WAS CRYING AND SCREAMING IN PAIN. SOMETHING HIT ME IN MY LOWER BACK. DALE THEN WRAPPED HIS LEGS AND FEET AROUND MY NECK IN A HEAD LOCK. DALE LET GO OF MY NECK AND BEGAN KICKING ME IN THE BACK WITH HIS FOOT. HE ALSO SLAPPED MY RIGHT SHOULDER AND AROUND MY UPPER BACK. HE SEEMED TO KICK ME EVEN MORE…. HE WAS DIGGING HIS FEET INTO MY BACK.

A MEDICAL EXAMINATION WAS CONDUCTED ON MISS LEGALLY ANNONYMOUS ON THE 8TH JUNE, APPROXIMATELY 60 HOURS AFTER INTERCOURSE. IT LASTED 45 MINUTES AND INCLUDED BOTH EXTERNAL AND INTERNAL VAGINAL INSPECTION. NO INJURY OF ANY KIND. MISS LEGALLY ANONYMOUS CLAIMED TO HAVE REPORTED INTERNAL PAINS AND INJURIES.
THE MEDICAL EVIDENCE DID NOT SUPPORT THIS.

If this attack was so brutal as she states, then you would think if true, a women would be upset and at home, but here's what she said in her statement which was then refuted line by line by her own prosecution witness that she had called onto the stand to back up what she said.

PERFECTED GROUNDS OF APPEAL PAPERS
MISS LEGALLY ANONYMOUS TOLD THE JURY THAT SHE AND MISS GREEN HAD BEEN SO FRIGHTENED BY APPELLANT AND THE RAT THAT SHE KEPT OUT OF WAKEFIELD AFTER THE "RAPE" TO AVOID SEEING THEM.
CONTRADICTED BY HER OWN STATEMENT AND BY THE EVIDENCE OF MISS GREEN THAT ON THE NIGHT OF 8TH JUNE 1994, COMPLAINANT AND GREEN IN WAKEFIELD FROM 11.20PM TO 2 AM IN NIGHTCLUBS AND EATING TAKEAWAY FOOD IN THE STREETS.

Again I don't think I need to point out the blatant absurdity of this. She had in one of her first statements said that her and Green had gone to a Jehovah witness meeting!

When in reality 48 hours after this so called brutal rape, she was out dancing and partying in nightclubs in the centre of Wakefield until 2 a.m in the early hours, then eating kebabs in the street. The bullshit of what I'm writing right now just blows my mind and again I have to say why wasn't the trial stopped and the charge thrown out at this very stage and her sent to the cells for perjury!

The second day ended, and I went back through the rigmarole of being escorted by Group Four back to HMP Armley. I felt a little more optimistic after what I'd seen in the courtroom and was looking forward to having my say in the morning, which was day three of the trial

There were always fitful nights of sleep in those cells. Like try, for example, putting this book down for five minutes and standing in the smallest room in your home. Just sit or stand in your bathroom, for instance, and try to imagine my cell and my innocence.

The morning of the third day I was put through the Leeds jail reception again, cuffed up and put in my little claustrophobic cubicle in the van and driven through the busy traffic towards the courts. I watched the normal people moving around through the plexiglass window from the van and hoped to the Gods I would soon be amongst them and away from this living nightmare.

As far as I remember I took the stand first that morning and swore an oath on the Holy Bible to tell the truth and nothing else. To which I recall thinking, when I said these words and looked at Judge Arthur Hutchinson, that I would tell the truth as I'd done from day one, and that it was about time the courtroom heard some truths. To that point all I had heard was blatant lies and clear perjury from **MISS LEGALLY ANONYMOUS'S** mouth.

I focused my gaze upon the jury when replying to the prosecutor's attempts at trying to make me look like I was lying. I didn't need to pause and think as I was telling the truth. I was on the stand a good hour getting grilled and I kept my composure and thought I gave an honest, coherent account of what had happened. Then my QC questioned me and made the obvious points to the jury about how I was telling the truth and that the evidence against me made no sense at all. The Rat went next and recounted his innocent actions that night.

Again the judge sided with the prosecution and had the jury dismiss most of the obvious points that had been made in our favour. Again I must stress the point that everything I said in my police statement matched what I said on the stand, unlike **MISS LEGALLY ANONYMOUS** who not only contradicted her own statement compared to what she said on the stand, but also her witnesses contradicted what she said in her statement too.

It was back to HMP Armley for me for the third night, and the next morning the prosecution went through more statements that again made no sense. On the night in question, at around 11 p.m. **MISS LEGALLY ANONYMOUS** had gone to a bloke's house to end, in her mind, her relationship with him. It turned out that from his statement she had turned up unannounced, and he denied that there was a relationship at all. He had, like us, just used her for casual sex and this was what my defence had been trying to say all along. She was a product of a one-night stand, and she had never held down a relationship and always caused problems for men when they rejected her demands to be her boyfriend.

When she had arrived back at her house that night she looked as if she had been crying a bit, and I remember asking her if she was okay. She said she was, but never mentioned that she had just broken up with the bloke who had been sleeping with her. That night he had told her to leave him alone, and that he wanted nothing to do with her again.

I'm pointing all this out because my QC felt the same way when forming a defence against her lies. It was obvious it upset her, and then after consensual sex with two other men that very night, had in the morning regretted what she had done and concocted her rape with the help of some prompting from Miss Green. She hadn't been raped. She was just a girl who looked for relationships in casual sex, and just because we left in the early hours, she hated us. And when they called the police, she was more than likely told that the Rat had this secret. Then it becomes at least clear in my mind just how this all snowballed out of control.

Again, I must state that the police knew of the Rat's secret and I'm assuming that meant the Crown Prosecution Service were also well aware of it too. The solicitors and anyone involved in our legal team must have been aware of it. So why wasn't I told about it? If I had known about it, I would have asked for that secret to be admitted into consideration by the jury and judge when viewing my case. It undermined my innocence greatly, as some people will assume the Rat's secret is an indicator to our combined guilt on that night. But it's nothing like that at all. As you can read there was zero evidence showing us as rapists on the night we slept with **MISS LEGALLY ANONYMOUS** and plenty of evidence to point toward our innocence. So why was all this overlooked? It was overlooked because of the Rat's secret, and this is the whole point of this book, and the point I'm making. I feel like a scape goat for something the Rat and the police were hiding.

There were other boyfriends mentioned on the fourth day, all of whom said the same thing. **MISS LEGALLY ANONYMOUS** wanted a relationship, they had not. She had caused problems with one of them and his girlfriend. The father of her child had left her and remarried. I think my QC, Rodney, said to me while on a legal visit that if only I had bought her flowers! Or it might have been Mr Batty, come to think of it, who said it. I got what he meant, but felt that a bunch of flowers should not have been needed to stop you ending up in a rape trial, when all you did is get your leg over one boring Sunday night. God, how I wish I'd never gone out or never gone down there in the first place. But I did, and I didn't do no wrong, so it was always difficult to blame myself for the circumstances I found myself in.

My mum had taken the stand and recounted her statement, recalling how I had told her I had met **MISS LEGALLY ANONYMOUS** before and that she had seen before the night in question the braid of hair she had given me when I'd first slept with her.

She was unhurt by the prosecution trying to make her out to be a liar. The judge again showed misdirection and bias by saying maybe she had just come to protect her darling boy!

Chapter 15

My fourth night in HMP Leeds was a tough night. I didn't sleep a wink for worrying. The whole long stretch of remand had swamped my mind all night and the silence of the wing when it had stopped all its banging had me stare out of the bars over into the skyline of the city and watch the dawn rise on a new day. It was judgment day and the fifth and final day of the trial, and I wondered just what the day had in store for my innocent bones.

A few of the wanker Armley reception screws said to me when I passed through that morning that they would see me at teatime, meaning they believed the courts would find me guilty. I had learned to keep my mouth shut, and I didn't want to cause a scene on the morning I was due in court, so I just smiled back at them and said sarcastically that I doubted it very much.

Quietly, I seethed thinking how they just didn't realise they were talking to an innocent young lad and I wondered how they would cope if thrown into the same nightmarish predicament. The van from Group Four got going through the early morning Leeds traffic, and I watched the people through the one-way window getting on with their mornings and I could smell freedom so close to being mine once again. I couldn't wait to go home, and my plan was to go out for a holiday to the Middle East and visit my dad who was out working near Dubai. It was thoughts of home and travel that had kept me sane along the rocky road of incarceration.

The usual palaver proceeded us in the cells at Leeds crown before getting us brought up into the courtroom. As the jury shuffled in and took their seats I scrutinised each face looking for a sign of hope, a sign of understanding, but most just kept a poker face and I couldn't tell how they were viewing me. There had been a couple of men on the jury in the earlier days of the trial that had given me a sympathetic smile as they adjourned for lunch. I had held on tight to these gestures, knowing that they all could see, and hear, we had not raped this liar. I've read and researched that a jury will feel you are guilty if you don't show remorse in your conduct in court! How the hell can you show remorse for something you have not done?

Most of the last day comprised of the prosecution and defences closing statements. I listened again as the prosecution tried their very best to paint this picture to the jury of these two brutal, sadistic rapists. It was hard to stand there and listen to it all. My QC, Rodney Jameson, and the Rat's QC, Tim Stead then gave it their all, showing we had committed no offence of rape. Lunch time came, and they took us down to the court cells to have a shit sandwich and coffee and then we were back up, and the afternoon proceeded with old Judge Arthur Hutchinson giving his summing up of the whole trial.

He made so many blatant mistakes during his summing up. He could have pointed out all the obvious points of law our defence teams had proved. The list was endless to what he could and should have said. All the times **MISS LEGALY ANONYMOUS** had contradicted her statement against what she said on the stand. It was clear as crystal perjury! All the evidence that pointed to her not being raped, like zero injuries, no actions showing any consistency of a woman who had been raped. Then all the obvious points we had proved. Telling the copper we had just had a threesome with a lass in (The estate she lived on). Going back to the house. Giving her a phone number to contact us again. Nothing added up. But the judge didn't say any of this. He waffled on for hours about the law and then told the jury it was not necessary to go over most of the trial points.

I could not believe what I was hearing, and as the jury went out to reach a verdict, they again sent us back down the stairs and into the cells to await the outcome.

Four hours later, they had come to their decision and as the court screws led us out of the cells, they both said that it was a good sign. They had heard quite a lot of the evidence because they had sat with us throughout the entire trial and had heard for themselves the bullshit. They both said to us we would go home soon.

It was a massive stress climbing those steps and entering the courtroom. Our families and friends were all in the public gallery and smiled over and gave a thumbs up and just tried their best to boost our confidence. Again, I think back to the Rat's discussion with me as they allowed us a quick visit under closed circumstances with our immediate family. After our mothers had left the quick visit, he had said to me, don't kick off if they come back with a guilty. I didn't want to think it could go wrong. From the very start we both knew we were not guilty of this charge, but so many things had gone against us up to that point, we just couldn't be sure anymore. I had told him I was going to go for the court doors and try to escape if I heard any guilty verdict. He talked me out of this the best he could, but I was certain in my mind that if they did this to me I was going to go for the door and try to break out of the court. In my mind, I thought I would escape the country and go to my dad. Yet again, I wonder back in hindsight to his worries, and why he even thought about getting a guilty. I was convinced we would walk free as we were innocent.

Chapter 16

Here they come. The jury, the people I didn't know from Adam who were about to free me from this absolute joke of a charge. There were a few moments where court assistants handed paper-work around the room, and I recall asking this usher if I could please have a glass of water. She looked at me like I was some kind of animal. She brought to me and not a decent gesture passed her face.

The judge spoke and addressed the jury; I heard the old bastard say,

"Have you reached a verdict?"

Then this guy in the front, who was the jury foreman, stood up and said to Judge Hutchinson that they had all reached a verdict. The judge then asked if it was a unanimous verdict to which the jury foreman again replied in the affirmative. At this point I would have thought they had seen the obviousness of all this crap, and all had come to the same conclusion and we were about to go free!

The judge said, "Can you read out your verdict for the court please."
and the jury foreman said, "Dale Brendan Hyde, on the charge of rape, we find you guilty!"

That was as far as the verdicts got. Over my left shoulder I noticed the Rat leap into action, racing over the benches where the solicitors and barristers were sitting, heading at full tonk for the judge.

It all happened so fast that, for several seconds I don't think anyone comprehended just what was going down. It also took me a second to comprehend just what was happening and for my own body to kick into fight-or-flight mode. The fighting would come later, so for now I joined the Rat in jumping over the dock and running into the centre of the courtroom. He then jumped across all the benches and onto the judges bench and was now brandishing a glass carafe of water at Judge Hutchinson, who, as I turned to run more towards where the doors to the court were situated, had fallen back in panic over his high-backed chair and disappeared beneath it as if he was looking for a place to hide. The court guards were now running towards the Rat and the Armley screws were hot on my tail as I focused on the double doors and freedom. The Rat's brother, J, ran from out of the public gallery right up in front of all the twelve puppet jury members shouting,

"She's a lying fat slag, they're innocent!"

It scared the jury to death, and all tried to get back to the door that led to their conference room. A friend of mine, Alan, who in all the confusion had come out of the public gallery too, got in my way and I had to sidestep around him. It was total chaos. Just at the beginning, as the Rat had made his first move at the sound of my guilty verdict, I had heard my mum burst into tears at the outcome.

The next thing we were both under a scrum of uniformed bodies and getting dragged roughly out of the court, back towards the cell area steps. I can't remember what happened to the Rat as he was nearer the Judge's bench, but he had shouted out in pain as the court screws roughed him up. I had my arms twisted so badly up my back that my wrists fractured. Once the screws from Armley had me through the door and out of sight of the courtroom, they really went to town. As they smashed my head into the railings on the stairs; it felt like I was about to lose consciousness. I'm not sure what put me out, but I remember waking up in a pool of blood and sick. Not sick, but like a pool of bile. I felt one of my eyes close and I couldn't see very well. I gathered myself onto the little bench that you can sit on in the cell and tried to figure out just what the fuck had happened! I shouted out a few times, calling the Rat to see if he was okay, but I heard nothing back. The corridors were empty of sound.

Around an hour later my cell opened, and I stared back at a few Armley screws and court guards. I was told my transport had arrived to take me back to prison, and another screw showed and made me sign some paperwork declaring that I was found guilty and that court is suspended because of the contempt, and that sentence would be postponed until a later date decided by Judge Hutchinson. I found out later that the Rat had received the same guilty verdict and that he too would return later along with me to find out our sentences.

It wasn't the Group Four van that awaited me now outside the enclosed compound area outside the cells of Leeds Crown Court. This screw from Armley cuffed his wrist to mine and shoved me out towards this saloon car. They placed me in the back seat, while this other screw got in the back, squashing me between them, and he also cuffed himself with another set of handcuffs to my other wrist. Another screw then got into the driver's seat and another into the passenger seat and we set off out of the controlled gate into the rush hour traffic of Leeds city centre, heading towards the house on the hill.

I sat numb between these two lumps. My mind was going a million miles an hour, but the traffic out of the car window seemed to be in slow motion. I even daydreamed a little and thought of the opening scenes to *MCVICAR* as they drive him out of the prison to *The Who* soundtrack blasting 'Free Me'.

But this was no movie set. My life had been destroyed with lies and I just couldn't accept what was happening. I entered the gates of HMP Armley in a total daze.

Chapter 17

The wanker screws that had said I'd be back were grinning in reception, yet I could tell it shocked them. News had spread on the prison grapevine about the chaos that had occurred in the courtroom. One of the long key-chain screws could see I was a little more than distressed, and thankfully he put me into a separate room while they figured out where I was going on the wing. I was now a convicted rapist in theory, yet I couldn't have been more innocent of the charge.

They classified me as an 'E' man, which was an escapee classification and classed as high-risk cat 'A'. They would have given me a prison uniform to wear, but as an 'E' man they gave me this blue and yellow patched together pair of joggers and sweatshirt. I could keep my own trainers though, as I had convinced the doctor that since my toes were broken playing football at Doncatraz, I'd needed to wear my own footwear. So they spared me the backi-tin shoes that quite a lot of the convicted had on their feet.

The reception screws explained how I would be held as an escapee prisoner and went through the loss of rights that came with the label. I had to wait for the screws to radio and get the dog handlers to escort me from one area to another. So I waited in this holding reception cell until the dogs came. It was nice to see an animal, but these were no friendly pet dogs. They looked menacing, and the owners who had them on short leashes looked even more so. I went to the middle spur on the ones, and then the PO came to speak to me to give me a lecture about how he wouldn't stand for any nonsense and that as long as I did as I was told I would be okay with him. His tone and attitude left no explanation necessary what I would get if I didn't behave. To be honest, at that point all the fight had gone out of me, I was so numb because of what had just happened at the Crown Court.

In a dream-like state, they took me up toward the higher landings by a gate that you could see through. About seven cells were in a row and as I passed, I noticed all the cards outside the cell doors had Cat 'A' on them. I was told to wait in front of the last cell in the row, and they placed my card into this little metal holder outside. It had on it, my name and Cat 'E' and my religion, which at the time was Roman Catholic.

The screw wrote in this little notebook where I had come from, and where in the prison I had moved to. The date and time added, and then I was told to enter the cell. It was quite a bare cell with whitewashed walls that gave it a cold feel. On the left was a small table and chair made from hardened cardboard, and then there was a small, low, single iron bed, which didn't have a mattress on it. The door slammed shut, and the screws walked away.

That silence in that cell was eerie. My world had become a total nightmare. Looking around my surroundings, my mind just couldn't focus away from the sound of "guilty" I'd heard coming from the jury foreman's mouth. The commotion afterwards seemed like I'd been involved in something that Leeds Crown Court had never seen before. I kept thinking how my family was feeling, knowing they would be worried sick about me. I wondered where the Rat was and how he was coping. Again, if I had known his secret, I wouldn't have given a shit about him. But back then I was missing a few pieces to this jigsaw made from a thousand pieces, which on the cover of the box, was a photo of a lying piece of shit.

The silence of my cell broke. I climbed up on the chair, which I'd dragged over to the barred window high up in my cell. I could hear a conversation between two black inmates taking place. From their accents I made them out to be local Leeds\Jamaican. The conversation had caught my attention because it was about me.

One of them was saying how he had read about my escape attempt at Leeds crown by seeing that evenings *Evening Post*. The other had replied that I was a rapist! To which the other had replied in return that something didn't sound right with the case. I wanted to shout out of my own window he was right, but as I was about to, my cell door suddenly flew open and a few screws stood there. I was told to get down from the window and told that if they caught me up there again, I'd be nicked.

They escorted me down to the ones landing and pointed in the direction of the server's hot plate to get my late food. On the 'A' category block we were all taken down one at a time. So I didn't really see much of anyone, and again that suited me just fine at that point. I ate my slop back in my cell and despised every rancid mouthful. That night one side of the wing was out for association, which was something I wouldn't be getting as an 'E' man.

A couple of nameless faces appeared at my metal door flap that evening, who I assumed must have been wing landing cleaners, as they had access to the locked part we were on and were curious to see who was locked up on this block of cells. No one spoke to me, which again suited me just fine.

It was a long night in that cell, the first night after being convicted. The screws had come to my door around 8 p.m. and told me to strip off my clothes, which would be folded and left outside my cell door until unlock in the morning. I had a pair of gym shorts and a vest to wear for the night. They also put my trainers outside.

All the chat out of the windows made me paranoid, thinking everyone was talking about me and this bullshit stigmatic crime. The night clocky had tapped on my metal and glass flap in my door around ten p.m. and I'd got up from my bunk and walked over to the steel door to see what he wanted. The night clocky was okay, asking if I was okay because it was obvious I was stressed out and that I should try to get some sleep. But he also mentioned something that got me thinking long into the night. He said he had seen outside one newsstand in the centre of Leeds, you know when they write the headlines on one of those sandwich board signs to draw you in to buy a paper, well; he had told me he had seen the statement on the *Evening Post* newspaper stating,

RAPISTS IN CROWN COURT ESCAPE BID FOILED!

That news just blew my mind and when he had gone on along the landing, shutting my steel flap on his way, I went and sat on my iron bed and thought just how many people had read about the end of the day at Leeds crown and our contempt for the mistaken guilt!

In the morning, the guvnor came to my cell, accompanied by several screws. He told me they would hold me on the 'E' list for twenty-eight days and then I would come up in front of him for review. I was then told by a senior officer that I could go out alone on exercise for one hour every day, weather permitting, and that I would be escorted to the prison library once a week where I could choose a few books.

I could also go to the office on the ones and use my phone card to make calls. These calls would be listened in on and recorded. And that was pretty much my lot as far as life went back then. I paced my cell floor and tried sleeping away the days for the first part of the week and then I got my chin up a little and I started doing cell exercises to strengthen me up and to keep my mind from turning into mush. I would do sit-ups in sets of fifty and then do fifty press-ups. I would then have a nosey out of the high set barred window and then lay on my bed for a while, thinking about the trial and my loved ones' back at home. I would then do some shadow boxing in my cell and then do a handstand up against the door and do press-ups from that position, which are called commando press ups.

Once I'd got my visit to the library, accompanied by a few screws with German Shepherd dogs, I would then bring a chapter on my bunk into my routine, alternating from exercise to reading. I would pace the cell floor constantly, from the back wall under the window to the steel cell door on the opposite side of the room. If you walk around seven paces and then walk back seven paces, you kind of get the idea of how much space I had to move around in.

A week after I'd been on the 'E' man list, I'd spoken to my mum on the phone and reassured her, the best I could, that I was okay and that the appeal would sort all this mess out. I'd had a letter from my briefs, and they were confident that my appeal would be heard. I wasn't so sure of their confidence, as the first appeal after a Crown Court sentence goes back to the original judge, and I was quite certain that old Arthur Hutchinson would not be very favourable to me after what had gone down in his courtroom! But it was some light in what looked like a very long, dark tunnel. So, I held onto whatever glimmer of hope shone my way. The solicitor letters arrived infrequently but gave me updates on the barrister's progress regarding the appeal. It felt as though everyone had forgotten about me, to be honest. I filled most of the hours of the day by staring at the walls and worrying how I was going to cope with the situation. I couldn't exercise all day and night obviously, but I continued to do what I could to avoid the 'watching the paint dry' effect.

A few days before my first review of being on the 'E' man list, which had been a long twenty-six days behind my cell door, I had a piece of string, nothing more than a foot long. It was about the thickness of a shoestring. I'd found it in the yard when I'd been out on exercise one day, and I'd pocketed it without thinking much about it. I'd used it to pass the time, tying knots that I could remember my dad showing me as a kid, as he had been in the fire brigade before his long career in the Middle East in the oil field. There was also a spare pair of shorts and a jumper to keep me warm, which one cleaner had sent me on the long line via the outside method of sending stuff through the windows.

So the night before my review, as they were taking out my gear, the screws started searching my cell and found these extra bits of stuff that shouldn't have been in my cell. They made a big show of putting it all into a clear prison bag and saying they would bring it up at the review meeting in the morning with the guvnor.

It was just another piss take, in the morning they took me with the dogs down to the guvnor's office and made me stand on a line on the floor with three screws stood around me as a shield to protect the guvnor as he spoke. He made a mountain out of a molehill regarding the string like it was a twenty foot rope with a grappling iron on the end and the shorts and jumper as if they were a black army camouflage fatigues or something of that nature. Arguing was pointless, as in his mind I'd concocted some kind of escape kit!

I was told I would not come off the 'E' man list, and that they would put me back behind my door for another twenty-eight days.

Chapter 18

I'd only had one visit from outside in the first month, as I was on closed visits and it was more stressing seeing my poor mum behind a glass screen, not being able to give her a hug or talk properly because you had to bend your head down to the corner of the glass where there was a gap to speak through. My long hair was gone, my head now shaved to the bone, which had added to the shock when my mum had seen me. The nurse in Armley bandaged my wrists, she didn't think I needed an X-ray but had taken some care in bandaging them tight. Again the piss-take with the shoestring piece of 'rope' that the guvnor had used to knock back my review over, made no sense as I could have used to more of an advantage all the bandages if I'd unwrapped them.

My mum was upset on the closed visit and I'd decided not to have any more until my visits got put to normal. Seeing my mum so upset in those surroundings made me hate **MISS LEGALLY ANONYMOUS** to my very core. I've hated her for many years, but now I just pity the sad bitch. It's her who has to live with the fact that she knows deep down that she made this bullshit up. She can pretend all she wants to the silly circle of friends that she has around her, but I know the truth and so does she. She makes out to be into God and all that, and I'm glad that the Lord will one day judge her for her sins.

So, I got my head down the best I could into the restricted routine of being held as an 'E' man. I had continued my exercise routine and was feeling stronger than I'd been when I'd been with the Rat in Doncatraz. My library visits had been good, and I'd got a few decent books that I'd wanted to read. I'd sit out on exercise when weather was sunny, which only added to my misery. The planes flying high above my head were now distant reminders of freedom. I'd watch the white trails of vapour hang in the air and dream of the day I would be on my way to the Middle East. Out of the blue around five or six weeks after the kick-off at court, they informed me I would be going back up in front of Judge Hutchinson for my sentence.

That was a bad night's sleep, as I wondered over and over in my mind just what he was going to give me. My legal visit with Mr Batty had left me with him hinting that I should expect around seven years! It was an amount of time I could not comprehend living through as a convicted rapist in prison when I was innocent.

In the morning I went through the rigmarole of being moved from my cell to reception and then to Leeds court under the strict monitored conditions of an 'E' man. I'd not seen the Rat for a good while and I remember thinking when we were both let out to go see our barristers before the sentence, that he looked frail and I knew then that it had been a good thing for me getting split from him. I felt stronger in myself, and the time spent exercising in my pad at Leeds had done me the world of good.

My feeling of strength soon turned to one of fear. In a small side room I sat listening to my QC, Rodney Jameson, telling me with obvious concern, that he didn't know what the judge was going to do. My heart fell into the pit of my stomach when he said that I should expect at least ten years, and with what had happened in the court on the last day of the trial, it wouldn't surprise him if he handed down a life sentence!

The time came when we were both called up in front of Judge Arthur Hutchinson. They were taking no chances this time with the pair of us and they cuffed us to a screw on either side with further screws in front and behind us as we climbed the stairs. Hutchinson entered the court with a look of hatred that had me believing what my QC had just said about copping for a life sentence. The judge revelled in the moment as he started slagging the pair of us off. He must have gone on for a good half an hour insulting us and calling us animals. He said that in his entire working life on the bench he had never heard of or seen a more blatant act of contempt of court in his very own courtroom.

Then he got ready to sentence us for the crimes, which he again informed us, they had found us guilty of. I had received strict instructions from my QC that no matter what he said or did; I was to accept it and to let him do his job in preparing and admitting the appeal.

My stress levels were so high at that exact moment in time, that as I looked towards the judge, his face seemed to turn in a trip-like way into a pig. That's how messed up my mind was at that moment. He sentenced me first, making a big show and pausing for dramatic effect, before saying, for the charge of rape they sentenced me to eight years in prison, with three more months to serve for contempt of court. He gave the Rat seven for rape, because he was younger than me, but evened it up by giving him a full year for contempt of court. I guess you don't attack Crown Court judges and receive a slap on the wrists.

So we trudged back down the stairs to the cells to await the vans to take us back to our separate prisons. I wouldn't see the Rat again for well over a year.

Chapter 19

The guvnor knocked me back a further three times, I'd gone up every twenty-eight days for review. No reasons given, and I'd stopped caring to be honest. I felt just the same as I'd felt while down the block in Doncatraz, and that a cell was a cell, and it didn't matter to me which cell they put me in until I was totally free. In my fourth month on the 'E' list I'd received a legal visit from Mr Batty, who told me that they had drawn my appeal papers up and would go up in front of Judge Hutchinson in Leeds very soon. So it was a hopeful bit of progress and I clung onto the hope of it with every fibre in my body.

In my fourth, monthly review of my 'E' man category status, the guvnor removed me from the list, and I was allowed out on association that night. I was a bit wary about mingling with the lads, but over the four months I'd had the odd decent person at my door and I'd told them all about the case and I'd spoken to most of the wing cleaners, as they were out and about on the wing most of the day and had been at my door a good few times. So there were a few friendly faces when I went and stood near the pool table and a few lads said, "alright". I got on the phone to my mum and a few mates from back home to tell them I was finally off the escape list. So I went back to my cell that night feeling rather good for the first time in a long time.

Things were not as they seemed though. In the morning I was outside my cell after coming back up from the breakfast server and I noticed this screw with a clipboard going around a few cells. I'd asked the cleaner near me what it was all about, and he had replied that it was a ship out list for HMP Walton up in Liverpool. I'd no sooner said to the cleaner that thank fuck I wasn't on that list, when the screw came wandering my way along the cells checking the cards outside that identified the occupants. The next moment he's asking while looking over at me, if I knew where Hyde's cell was? To which I said to him it was me he was looking for. He marched over and ran his finger down this list of names on his clipboard and then made a tick next to my name. He then gave me a sheet of paper detailing my imminent move to Liverpool the next day.

I'd heard only bad things about HMP Liverpool, and it was not the news I needed or expected. As soon as I had come off the escape list I was messed about and moved not only miles away but to a worse prison. I barricaded my door the best I could that night in protest, but in the morning they broke through and dragged me out and frog marched me down to reception. Just before they put me in the van for Liverpool with about ten other inmates from Leeds, the Rat's brother J, who was working down in the reception got over to talk with me and palmed me a nice chunk of cannabis resin for my journey onwards.

I felt sorry for J, as he had done nothing at court except to try to help, or what he thought was help. For his run out of the public gallery where he had shouted at the jury that she was a lying slag, he had been brought in front of Judge Hutchinson a few weeks after we had received our sentences, and had received a four month sentence for contempt of court. His defence solicitor had tried to argue that he had just started a new job and had had a new baby daughter recently, but the judge didn't give a shit and sent him to prison too. All these years later, as I write this, I can say that we don't get along anymore, but he never did me any harm and I only wish him well in life. It not his fault he has a Rat for a younger brother.

So the Group Four van pulled out of the old castle looking prison at the top of Gloucester Terrace, Leeds and headed onto the motorway towards scouse land.

It was a fair old journey in the back of the sweat box, and I wasn't exactly looking forward to reaching my new destination. I just felt I was going further away from my roots and my family, and it just made me feel that much more isolated than ever.

The first thing I noticed as they processed us into HMP Walton, was that in the reception holding area cell there was a massive written piece of graffiti that said,

WELCOME TO HELL!

It certainly wasn't far off the biblical threat.

Liverpool prison is a 1,370 capacity category 'B' men's facility, built in 1855. It has quite a chequered history, for example. In February 1939, the IRA attempted, but failed, to break a wall of the prison during the S Bomb campaign in Britain that year. In the Liverpool blitz of World War 2 on September 18, 1940, German high explosive bombs falling on a wing of the prison partially demolished it, killing twenty-two inmates. The body of one was only found eleven years later when they cleared the rubble.

The prison was the site of sixty-two judicial executions from 1887–1964. In May 2003, some eight years after I was held there, her majesty's chief inspector of prisons compiled a report severely criticising it for its overcrowding. The inspection had found that parts of the jail were unclean, had cockroach infestations, broken windows, and inmates could only shower and change their clothes once a week!

A further inspection in 2010 stated that drugs, bullying, and violence were still prevalent. So, as you can read, it wasn't a very nice new home for me to live in. Back in 1995 it still didn't have electricity or toilets. It was slop out for a poo and batteries for your radio. There was still evidence of the bombing from the war in places too, with large mounds of red brick rubble scattered around the prison grounds. They put me into a basic rundown cell, and I was basically told to just get on with it. The whole prison seemed overrun with heroin addicts, and throughout the day and night, all I could hear out of my cell window was the scouse dialect shouting, one junkie to another,

"Send mi a line la." Or "Av ya got eny gear mayte." Or even, "Sort it lad, sort it kidda."

Chapter 20

I got books from the library about law, trying to look for some answers that might help my appeal. I discovered my favourite writer in Liverpool prison. Brendan Behan had been an inmate himself once in the 1940s over his IRA activities. I came across his debut novel, *Borstal Boy,* while rooting through the library shelves. After about three months in there, I had a legal visit from Mr Batty telling me that the appeal would be heard that week in front of Judge Hutchinson. It was a crucial time, and I prayed that he would finally see sense and free me. I'd had some family visits from my mum and sister and a few friends before this legal visit, but again, I'd told them to not worry too much about travelling all that way and that writing letters was a nicer and easier way to communicate. But my mum, bless her, kept travelling up for visits and she deserves a medal for her love and loyalty.

I'd written letters to the prime minister and to my MP, but I'd heard nothing back at that point. I'd also written to the charity, Liberty, asking for help, but they had replied with a letter stating that because I already had a legal team working on my behalf, they couldn't get involved.

I had shown a few inmates my depositions, and after they had read through my case, they had all come back to me and said I shouldn't be in here. I used my head and gave my 'deps' to some of the most notorious inmates, who passed on their opinion of my case to their pals, who then spread it to their pals. So, I had quite a lot of the lads on my side in there, knowing an innocent man walked amongst them. I still got the odd idiot giving me shit, and I had to endure the nameless, faceless, shouting out of the cell windows on a night where someone would just start calling me a beast or a rapist or a sex case.

But to be honest, I grew such a thick skin while I was inside that most of it just went over my head. I was about to get my appeal hearing, and I was sure again in my heart that I was on my way home soon.

It was the principal PO screw who called me into his office a week later and told me he had just had confirmation via my legal team that my appeal had been denied! Dejectedly, I left the office in a world of pain, wondering how the system could allow this to happen. My mind went into a very dark space for quite some time after that. I think a turning point came for me when, one day, my mail slid under my cell door and there was a bright red envelope amongst the white envelopes. I opened it and removed a card from my mother that had on the front a poem by Rudyard Kipling called 'IF'.

If you can keep your head when all about you

Are losing theirs and blaming it on you,

If you can trust yourself when all men doubt you,

But make allowances for their doubting too;

If you can wait and not be tired by waiting,

Or being lied about, don't deal in lies,

Or being hated, don't give way to hating,

And yet don't look too good, nor talk too wise:

If you can dream—and not make dreams your master,

If you can think—and not make thoughts your aim;

If you can meet with Triumph and Disaster

And treat those two imposters just the same;

If you can bear to hear the truth you've spoken

Twisted by knaves to make a trap for fools,

Or watch the things you gave your life to, broken,

And stoop and build 'em up with worn-out tools:

If you can make one heap of all your winnings

And risk it on one turn of pitch-and-toss,

And lose, and start again at your beginnings

And never breath a word about your loss;

If you can force your heart and nerve and sinew

To serve your turn long after they are gone,

And so hold on when there is nothing in you

Except the Will which says to them: "Hold On!"

If you can talk with crowds and keep your virtue,

Or walk with kings—nor lose the common touch,

If neither foes nor loving friends can hurt you,

If all men can count with you, but none too much;

If you can fill the unforgiving minute

With sixty seconds' worth of distance run,

Yours is the Earth and everything that's in it,

And—which is more—you'll be a Man, my Son!

It made me cry reading this from my mum, but it made me also get up out of the depression that had swamped me since losing the appeal at the hands of Judge Hutchinson and make me fight back even harder. From that moment on I got back into an even more rigorous regime with my training, doing my cell exercises again and reading everything I could from the prison library on law. One of the worst things that happened regarding losing the appeal was not only my freedom, but because they had knocked the appeal back, I had now lost my legal aid!

My mum and dad had both written to me regarding this and said that they were both there to support me financially. My mum had said that she was going to speak to the Rat's mum about going halves regarding paying to send one of the QC's down to London to see if we could get granted a hearing at the Court of Appeal on the Strand.

So, I waited out my time and tried my best to keep the dark thoughts at bay. It was difficult sometimes, even with a good routine. The depth of the situation had me feeling like I was at the bottom of a cavernous hole, trapped and small and with no tools to even contemplate the climb upwards. Every time I entered my cell, I'd glance at my ID card in its little holder outside my door. The '8 year 3 months' written upon it just seemed like it had nothing to do with me, yet the cold, hard, steel door would bang behind me and I'd bunker down in my cell for another long day and night of misery and false imprisonment.

Chapter 21

A week or two later I received a letter from my mum saying that she had spoken to the Rat's mum and that she had said they couldn't afford to pay for a barrister to represent The RAT! Myself and all my family thought this very strange, because we would do anything to take the case to the High Courts in London. It was a few grand, but even if it had been a hundred grand, my mum and dad would have sold their homes to set me free. They didn't doubt my innocence and were fully behind me regarding getting the case heard by higher judges at the Royal Courts of Appeal. So, again, I must point out why would the Rat's mum and family not find the cash to help him? Did his mum know something about him I didn't back then? I'd say it's obvious they knew the Rat's secret.

So my family paid the fees for Rodney Jameson, QC, to go down to London to represent me, which in theory, because the Rat was my co-accused, meant that if I got released, he would also be released. gain, Back then I didn't read too much into his family not being willing to support his fee to get the case heard at the High Court, and it wasn't again until over a decade later that I realised just why they hadn't supported him. It was clear at the time to me though, that it made little sense regarding them being skint. My mum wrote to me in anger saying that, not much later she had bumped into the RATS mum and she had just bought a newish car. My mum had said she looked sheepish when they had met, and my mum just walked away thinking what a disgrace they were as a family.

For me, the seasons outside in the yard changed and the view from my cell window, if I climbed up, did too. But my day-to-day life didn't really change much. Then suddenly, I was on the move again. This time to HMP Birmingham's Winson Green. Another shit-hole of a nick.

A month earlier I'd had some dental problems and the facilities at Liverpool were just not equipped to deal with the matter, so they had said I needed to go back to Leeds for the dentist there to do it. I guess they could have taken me to an outside dentist, but cuffed up and under escort, it seemed an easier thing for them to shove me on the G4S van and send me to Leeds for a few days, and then have me returned.

The journey down to Birmingham wasn't too bad. I'd heard only bad things about Winson Green. In 1999, three years after I was there, the inspection report, from her majesty's chief inspector of prisons, attacked conditions at HMP Birmingham, describing the health centre in the jail as the "untidiest and dirtiest" inspectors had ever come across. Also mentioned in this report were inadequate bathing arrangements, where some inmates were only being allowed a full wash three times a week, which I guess sounds bad, but it was better than Liverpool. When I was there, it was a shower and kit change just once a week. With slop out and the massive heroin problem and the cockroaches, it stunk like the Victorian hell hole it always had been.

In March 2001, the chief inspector declared that conditions had worsened in Birmingham Prison, where around eleven per cent had claimed to have been assaulted by prison officers. It's not a claim, it's a fact. And the percentage was probably higher, but a lot of inmates, me included, just didn't bother reporting the abuse. It just all seemed part and parcel of life back then in the big prisons.

Many judicial executions by hanging took place at the prison until they abolished capital punishment in the UK. The first was that of Henry Kimberley, on St Patrick's day 1885, for the murder of Emma Palmer, God bless her. Thirty-five executions took place at Birmingham Prison during the twentieth century. The last person ever to be hanged at the prison was a twenty-year-old Jamaican named Oswald Augustus Grey. They executed him on 20 November 1962, after being convicted of the shooting to death of newsagent, Thomas Bates, God bless him, during a robbery.

There have been a few famous inmates over the years in Birmingham such as Konon Molody, aka Gordon Lonsdale, Soviet spy, involved in Spy Swap. Charlie Wilson imprisoned for his part in the great train robbery. He escaped the prison on 12 August 1964. They recaptured him on 25 January 1968, in Canada. Ozzy Osbourne, front man of the heavy metal band *Black Sabbath*. He served 6 weeks in 1966 for breaking and entering and theft. Michael Collins, Irish revolutionary, spent a short period in the prison after the Easter rising of 1916. The Birmingham 6 were freed after the worst miscarriage of justice in the country. And the horrible bastard Fred West, who killed many, including his own family.

It's this beast I will mention the most, as when I'd arrived at the prison, the screws in charge at Birmingham were refusing to let me go on normal location, because with my charge they felt I would be in serious danger. They offered protection on the nonce wing, which I totally refused. So I ended up going down the block as a compromise. It was while I was down here that I heard just how Fred had been acting and the full horror of his crimes. A chatterbox night clocky who always stopped at my block cell door on a night gave me the low down. As Fred took so many lives, it shouldn't come as too much of a surprise that he took his own. His suicide in Birmingham Prison stunned the country at the time, and deprived millions who had been horrified in equal measure by the gruesome details, of seeing justice served upon him by the courts. HMP Winson Green had been his home for ten months since his arrest and the charge of murder of twelve women. They found their remains buried under the patios and foundations of his home. The fifty-two-year-old was the most notorious British prisoner by the time he arrived in February 1994.

His home in Cromwell Street, Gloucester, was the scene of a massive excavation by police and lots more chilling evidence was emerging about its macabre secrets. West's face was all over the front pages of most papers for many weeks, with former friends and past acquaintances dishing the dirt on his strange character. Yet it was his time on remand on 'D' wing that gave perhaps the most telling insight into just what made him tick.

Officially, he was prisoner WN-3617, but to the other prisoners they knew him as 'The Digger'. He acquired this nickname as soon as he landed in the prison. As a top security remand prisoner, he was in a cell on his own and given the same protection as a sex offender amid fears that he could become a trophy victim for violent inmates who wanted to attack him. The Rackham's Slasher, David Morgan—on remand for the assault of ten women in a busy Birmingham department store—was just four cells away from West. But it was West who posed the greatest danger to himself. He was known to be very depressed, and to behave irrationally, but the authorities did not believe he would kill himself and cheat the courts from punishing him for his despicable crimes.

His records from previous spells at her majesty's pleasure showed that he had a long-standing fear of prisons, but there was no reason to suspect that it might drive him over the edge. Instead, he gave every impression of settling into the routine of prison life, going as far as making it a home from home, complete with his own set of curtains and bedding!

The case was so vast against him he spent most of his time in interview sessions with detectives or his legal team. When he wasn't being interviewed, he used his limited English abilities to write a book about his crimes, even though it was unlikely to be published. His son, Steve, revealed to journalists that his father had the reading and writing age of a ten-year-old child. Fred's relaxation time was lying around smoking roll-ups and fretting about his house and pet goldfish.

His jovial nature and lack of concern for what he had done struck his fellow prisoners, and he seemed to remain at ease despite his growing infamy. There was no change in his behaviour or routine to suggest that anything was about to trigger his suicide. But inside, West was cracking up. He spent New Year's Eve playing pool and watching television. New Year's Day began with him eating breakfast. After lunch, just before he was due to be opened up to put his metal meal tray outside his door, the screws found him hanging in his cell. There was an attempt to resuscitate him, but after twenty minutes the prison doctor pronounced him dead.

He had asphyxiated himself by wrapping an improvised rope he had constructed from a blanket and tags he had stolen from prison laundry bags, around his neck, then he bound this device to a door handle and window catchment and sank to his knees.

At the bottom of the suicide note, later found in his cell, was a drawing of a gravestone upon which he wrote, "In loving memory. Fred West. Rose West. Rest in peace where no shadows fall. In perfect peace he waits for Rose, his wife."

The lads in the prison upon hearing about his death had cheered for hours and parties were had in the cells all night to celebrate the good riddance of such scum.

It turned out that I didn't even get to go to Leeds as they had told Birmingham that they had lost my medical file! So I spent a week in Winson Green down the block for nothing and soon found my way back to Liverpool, toothache in situ.

Chapter 22

Nine more long months pass and I guess the only thing that stands out was one day walking outside my wing in the prison grounds. I can't remember where I was going to or from, but I'd been at the back of a smallish group when out of the blue this screw, who was walking us, must have been bored with his day and picked me out, shouting at me to pick up my pace and hurry the fuck up. I think now I recall it was on the way back from Sunday chapel for the Roman Catholic religion. I'd replied that I was walking just as fast as everyone else, when suddenly I heard him run up behind me and shove me as hard as he could in the back, which sent me flying as I was off balance and not expecting it. I got to my feet and asked him what his fucking problem was when he said to his screw mate, who had a German Shepherd dog on a leash, to let it loose. This beast came flying at me at full speed and all I could do was turn my back on it to stop it jumping up at my face. It settled for biting into my left calf and clamped on for dear life while growling like a maniac.

The screw who had pushed me just laughed, and it took them a while to come and get the bloody thing off me. I spent the next month down the block for that, guilty of threatening an officer and insolence. I didn't get a month straight out, but every time they said I could go back on the wing I'd just told them to go fuck themselves and they had slammed the block door on me telling me to suit myself. I'd then be back up in front of the guvnor and given more block days.

After around a month, I stopped carrying on and got back up onto the wing. I'd had a visit off my mum and Grandma Betty, and they had both looked worried at my appearance from the month down the chokey. I remember my gran bless her shouting at this screw before she left the visits hall, saying how disgusted she was with the lot of 'em for setting the dog on me.

I gave my mum something on the visit that I'd made her while I did my block time. I had still received a bang up wage of a few quid and instead of buying tobacco or munch; I had bought this bag of matchsticks and glue and some card for design, which all came in one package and cost about the same as the full amount of bang up cash I had.

It had killed much precious boring time sat down the block at Walton and I'd had plenty of time to think and reflect on the Kipling poem 'IF' my mum had sent me with her card before.

I had cut my cardboard carefully, crafting a shape to glue my cut matches around as a border. They had allowed me my colouring pens from my property because I'd been down the block a while, and with those I drew vines of bright green with coloured leaves and flowers in an array of bright colours. I then spent days doing draft after draft of my poem for my mum and then carefully writing it all out inside the card in italics. I've still got it to this day, and it's as powerful now as it was back then. I will include it here for you to decide whether it was the thoughts and feelings of a young man stuck in a hellhole of a jail for a crime he didn't commit or the musings of a brutal rapist?

LOOK AND SEE THROUGH MY
WINDOW

BEARING INTO MY SOUL

LOOK AND SEE ALL THE TOMMOROWS

THAT NOW LAY DEAD AND OLD

IT'S TIME TO SEE THE PROOF

THE TIME TO REVEAL THE TRUTH

IT'S THE TIME NOW FOR SOME PEACE

SURELY MY RELEASE

LOOK AND SEE THROUGH THE
SHADOWS

AT THE DARKENING GLOOM

LOOK AT ALL THE HOURS SINCE IV'E
BEEN HOME

IT WON'T BE LONG NOW TILL I'M NO
LONGER ALONE

IT'S TIME FOR A NEW WORLD

IT'S TIME FOR MY DREAM

HOME WITH YOU MOTHER

JUST LIKE THE OLD TIMES USED TO BE.

My mum wrote me back when she received this and said I would be home soon. She also said that on her last visit as she was leaving Walton, a screw who she described as having very bright blue eyes had pulled her to one side just before the gatehouse and had asked,

"Are you Dales mum?"

She had told him that, yes, she was, and he had said to her,

"He shouldn't be in here".

I knew who she meant as he had asked to look at my depositions and I'd given him them to read. Quite a few screws seemed to be a little more polite toward me after he had given them back to me a few days later. I'd had the same reaction from everyone I'd given them too, after they had also read through the bullshit and lies.

My second Christmas had passed behind the prison walls, and my mood was low on those special days as I thought of not only what I was missing with family celebrations but also how there was an obvious empty chair around the Christmas dinner feast. There had been heavy snowfall on the prison yard at Walton and it had given some slight release, as it changed the usual dull scene into a blanketed white affair for a while.

The prison had got back to its normal routine in January, with again the night banged up in your cell being a hard time on New Year's Eve. I made a wish to thin air in my cell that night, hoping that soon they would grant my appeal in London. Some fireworks had gone off outside the prison walls and I caught sight of a few flashes of reds and greens bursting into shapes in the air, but it soon fizzled out and the empty, quiet cell was how my new year started.

During the second week of January, I received a legal visit from my QC. He handed me the perfected grounds for appeal that we would use in London to fight the case as soon as a date was confirmed.

For my birthday present that year, on 21 January, they called me into the Principal PO office. There were a few screws in the office with him who seemed to hate me because of my conviction, as if he had to make sure I felt intimidated. They couldn't stand telling me the news that my appeal hearing had been granted. I was elated, and read the form he gave me with a smile on my face., Because I had read through the perfected grounds of appeal written by my QC at the time, Rodney Mellor Maples Jameson, who, as I've mentioned is now Judge Jameson. I felt sure that this time the high lords and judges would see that this case was bullshit and that I would be acquitted and freed.

There was a very serious part of this form to sign, and again I ask you, the reader, to consider if you were guilty would you bother signing it? Part of the conditions of going down to London to appear in front of the Royal Court of Appeal Judges is that if they turned down the appeal, I would have to start my sentence from that date. So, the few years I had already served, would be for nothing. They also made it clear in this part of the form that if they thought my sentence too lenient, then they could increase it as they saw fit. It was a slight worry, as my faith in the system had been let down badly, but I knew I had to proceed and get my case in front of the High Court big-wigs.

After I had finished signing my forms and told to leave the office by the PO, one screw said it was pointless as I'd be back. He reminded me of the wanker Armley screw who had said before my trial that I'd be back at Leeds that teatime. I thought, as I walked out of the office, that he would be wrong this time and I knew in my heart that if there was any justice left in this great country of ours that they would free me.

Chapter 23

I said goodbye to a few lads who I had spoken to down the block and one screw let me give most of my stuff to my pal, who had chatted to me most nights through the pipes. He was a good scouse\Irish lad named Kildare. I was glad to get away from a few of my neighbours, though. One was nick-named 'Jigsaw'. One day, he had casually strolled into the local police station with a carrier bag and pressed the buzzer for attention. When they had come out, he had said they ought to have a look in the bag. It would have been quite a shock for whichever copper looked in, as the bloke had his wife's head in there. He had sawn it off with an electric saw, for fuck's sake.

There was also this armed robber, who was a proper hard case, but the thing is he had a pair of massive tits and long blonde hair. He was just left alone by the screws because it meant a quieter life for them if they just let him be. He made skirts out of pillow slips and had a screw bring him the chalk from the wing pool table, so he had on this bluish looking eyeshadow. It was quite a strange sight at night-time, as they let us all go for hot water. Seeing these types pass your door was something I will never forget.

So I left most of my accumulated belongings there, as we saw it as bad luck to take them all down to the appeal courts. Maybe it was just a way for the cons to grab a few bits for themselves out of your collection, but I didn't care and gave most of it away gladly. I wanted to be light of baggage as I moved to London. I had kept reading my appeal papers and was confident with what I was reading from my QC, Rodney. He had put together an excellent appeal with the errors from the trial. I had also had a letter from the appeal court itself stating that my appeal was being heard on 11 February and that it would take five days until the 15 February. What caught my attention the most in this letter was where they stated that the matter should, in their opinion, be expedited! Now back then I didn't know what that word meant, so I had asked for a dictionary and looked it up.

Expedite—Verb Make an action or process happen sooner or be accomplished more quickly.

So I felt even more confidence as the day drew near to head to The Strand in London.

It was a bitterly cold day when I was woken up and taken down to the reception holding cells for my trip south. I was nervous as hell, but also very upbeat, and I remember singing some of my favourite songs the whole morning, like John Lennon's 'Watching the Wheels', and Otis Redding's '(Sittin on) The Dock of the Bay'. The screws didn't even tell me to pipe down, which I took as a good sign that they were aware I should be free. It was a Saturday when they took me down, as my appeal trial started on the Monday, so I would be in Brixton for a week.

We had all heard on the radios around the prison at Liverpool about the enormous IRA blast that had exploded on the Friday, the day before I was to travel. The London Dockland bombing occurred when the provisional Irish Republican Army (IRA) detonated a powerful truck bomb in South Quay. The blast killed two people and injured a further one hundred. It was an enormous bomb that destroyed a wide area and caused around an estimated £150 million worth of damage. I started my journey into the capital the day after this 3,000 pound bomb had gone off. Unbeknown to us all, they would plant another bomb on the very last day of my hearing.

It was a long old ride from Liverpool to London in the slow Group Four van. Sat hunched up with my hands on my knees, I stared out of the little plastic one-way window at the cars and trucks on the motorway. About an hour into the journey, I noticed this sports car pull alongside the van, with the driver's passenger window directly in line with my window. I could see it was this business lady with long, dark-hair, dressed in a short skirt and stockings and a suit jacket. I couldn't see her face, but as she changed gear to zoom past the van, her skirt rode up a little as her leg hit the clutch and I caught sight of her lacy stocking top. It was a sight I had not seen in a long time, and it aroused me for a moment. When she had driven past, I thought about how a woman had caused me so much trouble. I wondered how I would regard women after all this had happened. Would I even be able to trust again ever or feel comfortable enough to make love to a girlfriend again? It was a real deep thought, and it became an issue much later in my life.

It's a 230 mile journey from Liverpool to Brixton, and I'd say in a decent car at a decent speed it would take you about four and a half hours. The sluggish Group Four van took about six hours. I remember passing through Warrington on the M6 and thinking of my elder brother who comes from there. I remember seeing Stafford signs on the motorway and thinking we were at least half-way there; I guessed.

Through Birmingham and Milton Keynes and on through Abingdon and Slough. I was desperate for the toilet at this stage and the van stopped at this small service stop. They also needed some petrol. The screw who let me out of the cubicle would normally tell me to put one arm out of the small gap so he could handcuff me to himself. He didn't! Opening my door and, he said, "Come on then." I remember jumping down off the bus step and feeling all weird and out of sorts. I'd not been in a normal outside setting for a long time and to see folks just getting on with filling their cars up with petrol spun my head a little. The screw walked me half-way to the service station doors and pointed out the sign and way towards the men's toilets. Setting off I thought how Group Four had allowed me to use a toilet un-cuffed at the motorway services. It would be easy to escape and I also felt like they wanted me to try, but I went for a piss and came straight back out to the van. I would not jeopardise my High Court appeal hearing and become a fugitive. I was going home legit and a free man, not looking over my shoulder as an escapee.

The van moved on after they had secured me back inside my cubicle, and I noticed signs for Heathrow Airport and hoped to God I would fly out of there soon to the Middle East to see my dad in Abu Dhabi. I had a good look out of the window as the van hit Kensington. The swanky houses made me sit up in awe as they seemed ever so majestic after the gloomy buildings I had lived in for the past two years and more.

It soon though got a little rough looking out the window, as I passed the districts of Nine Elms and Parsons Green and Battersea. We were soon at the turn onto Jeb Avenue, which is where the formidable HMP Brixton is situated. My nerves were twitching a bit as the van got ready to enter through its imposing gates.

The prison was built in 1820 and opened as the Surrey House of Corrections. They intended it to house only 175 prisoners, but overcrowding was an early problem and with its small cells and poor living conditions contributing to its reputation as one of the worst prisons in London. That reputation only increased, as a year later it introduced the dreaded treadmill into its system. It was a women's prison in its early years, and in 1852, after Van Diemen's Land (Tasmania) refused anymore prisoners from England under the penal transportation process, it expanded to house over 800 prisoners. Through the nineteenth century, conditions improved a little, but if you read the last few decades of reports from the chief inspector of prisons, Brixton still has serious modern day issues. From major concerns over spates of suicides and attempts to the disturbing report on how prison officers had sabotaged the inmates call bell, so it didn't ring while they were on their shifts. Staff had also sabotaged records relating to the inspector's report, falsifying information to make the prison look better than it was. Further reports concluded that many inmates were taking drugs, and that this was leading to many violent attacks between gangs inside the prison. The inspection also claimed that vermin infested the entire prison.

There have been some notable famous faces pass through HMP Brixton over the years. Oswald Mosley, founder of the British Union of Fascists, was interred in 1940 under defence regulation 18B. Gerard Tuite, a former senior member of the IRA, escaped the prison in 1980, along with London gangster and hitman Jimmy Moody. Other suspected IRA members such as Nessan Quinlivan and Pearse McAuley escaped in 1991. Even Mick Jagger of the rolling stones had done a bit of time inside Brixton for his pot bust in the 60s. I guess the most infamous characters held there were the Kray twins, Ronald and Reginald, held there in the early months of their famous trial that saw the pair each receive a thirty-year sentence. It became a military prison from 1882–1898 and remained a remand and trial prison until 2012. The footings for the treadmill remain and are visible and the former hanging cell\execution chamber is now an enlarged six-man cell.

Chapter 24

As they put me through reception with a large group of lads all arriving back from different courts all around London, a screw came and pulled me aside and said I had best keep my head down while they got the majority processed through and onto wings. They put me in a large room with about forty lads, about ninety per cent of them were black lads. We were told to get changed into our remand clothes, as we had all undergone a strip search upon re-entering the facility. I'd gone and sat on a bench near lots of these black lads and just tried to look like I was minding my own business, when I noticed across the room this white lad staring right at me. I minded my business and continued to get dressed.

"What ya in for mate?"
"Rape", I answered back.

To which this obvious trouble causing wanker replied,

"Ya better be fuckin' kidding!"
"I've been stitched up, down here for my appeal."
I added with a bit more venom in my voice this time

The lad who stood with an obvious crew of mates, looked over at me and I could tell he was weighing up the scene and getting ready to attack. I was ready to defend and annihilate this wanker, but before any need for violence went down, this huge black fella who sat a few seats down from me on this bench, just stood up and said to this white lad,

"Shut the fuck up and sit down, now."

He must have been respected, because all these white lads looked sheepish and sat back down and carried on putting on their socks, not daring to look up. When we got called out in groups to get put on wings, I was in the group with this big black fella and I thanked him for his intervention. He said he knew how it felt to be stitched up and wished me well for my appeal. They put me on a normal location wing and padded up with this skinny black Tottenham lad up for appeal for murder. It didn't faze me he was in for an alleged murder. Over the years from my robbery charges that I was guilty for, I had banged up a few times with killers.

I swept the landings and toilets out on the Sunday morning and I felt calm. I worked away methodically and hoped that these three High Court judges were going to put a stop to whatever mistakes had gone before, which me found guilty of a crime I didn't do. It wasn't only a crime I didn't do but one I feel strong about when it comes to real beasts getting punished and genuine victims getting the support and justice they so rightly deserve. Its why being labelled and wrongly convicted and slandered and abused over the years has hurt me deeply.

I had this fantastic black and white sketch of Bob Marley, one of the few nice bits of my belongings I had kept back and not given away in Liverpool. So, while on my cleaning job, I found the cell of the big fella who had stuck up for me in reception and slid it under his door without saying anything or opening his flap so he could see me. He was no fool though and shouted out through his door, "cheers and good luck at the royal."

Late that Sunday evening, after we had all been well and truly banged up behind the doors, this Tottenham lad who was sharing my cell said to me that if he came back after his appeal that he wouldn't be so friendly! I took this to be a veiled threat and told him that if I didn't get out by Friday and came back into this cell, I would be up for murder too. I wasn't going to take no shit of this fucker, and I went to bed wound up and ready to just get to the courts and get my justice before I did something I'd regret.

I had my breakfast in Brixton nick and soon found my way onto the van and before long I was looking out at the slow moving London traffic. I'd not seen the outside so much in ages, and it felt like a good omen that I would soon breathe free air once more. So it was Monday 12 February 1996 when the van pulled in off the Strand Road and drove through into the area of the Royal Courts of Justice where you disembark if you're in cuffs.

I was booked in by some serious-looking staff members and taken down these stairs to what I can only describe as a dungeon looking cell. In the reception, before I had gone down to the cells I'd seen and spoken to the Rat who had been brought from Castington Young Offenders Institution. They had moved him there while the appeal trial proceeded. They had put us in a reception holding cell before taking us down to the cells. It was strange seeing him again. It was a good year since the kick-off at Leeds Crown Court. We had on our own clothes too, so it felt strange looking at each other. We looked like we were ready for a night out, never mind the royal courts. The Rat said to me I looked well and fit, and I said cheers, but thought being away from him, I had done much better in adult prison and I definitely looked the healthier of the two of us. I'd put on a good bit of weight and was toned from my cell workouts. He, on the other hand, still looked like a stick thin rake and his dark baggy eyes told me he had continued with the gear.

A good half hour passed and then we were taken down into the cells to await the start of proceedings. It was nerve-wracking down there and the temperature was freezing, which didn't help the tension in the body. The cell door creaked open, and these guards told us to follow them up. I walked first up these worn green wood steps and as the little door at the top opened; I clocked the High Court interior for the first time, it was a dominating scene, let me tell you. I first noticed my QC, Rodney Jameson, down in some kind of pit. I was up high on a kind of balcony, like being at the theatre. The three high judges' chairs were over to my left, yet there was a gap of air between us of some twenty or thirty feet. They were just below in the pit area, shuffling paperwork and chatting between my barrister and the clerks of the court. I also noticed, that right at the back of the court on the ground floor, way over to my right, the detective in charge of the case, Detective Mc DX, sitting beside another man.

Proceedings soon got under way and the clerk said something and the guard who had told us to sit on this little wooden bench nudged me and said get up.

"All rise for His Honour Lord Staughton, His Honour Judge Macpherson, and His Honour Judge Gower."

The look from the three of them combined, once they had taken their throne-like chairs, was intimidating to say the least.

Chapter 25

Sir Christopher Staughton was a very distinguished judge who was first called to the bar by the inner temple in 1957. After developing a busy practice at the commercial bar as a tenant at the highly regarded three Essex Court Chambers, he took silk in 1970 and then became a Judge in the Queen's bench division in 1981. He was elevated to the royal Court of Appeal in 1987. Having resigned—not retired—a difference which he always underlined, from the Court of Appeal in 1997, he continued afterwards to act as arbitrator in many complicated contests. Staughton's formidable intellect was evident at an early age. He won a scholarship to Eton in 1946 and another to Magdalene College, Cambridge, where he won the coveted George Long prize for Roman law. He also became an honorary fellow of the college and held a further honorary degree from the University of Hertfordshire, the county in which he lived. He was born, Christopher Stephen Thomas Thayer Staughton, the son of Simon Staughton of Melbourne, Australia, and Madeline Jones of Halifax, Nova Scotia. It was a marriage which ended bitterly when he was still a small child, so bitterly in fact that he became a ward of the court!

However, he himself had a long and happy marriage, marrying Joanne Burgess in 1960. Staughton was conscripted into the army in 1953, becoming a second lieutenant in the 11th Hussars and was also a member of the Senate of the Inns of Court and was president of the Court of Appeals in Gibraltar. He died aged 81 in October 2014.

The second highest ranking judge to be glaring at me for the scheduled five days was Sir William Alan Macpherson. He had been called to the bar in 1952. From 1962 to 1965 he was a member of the Special Air Service, within the territorial army, holding the appointment of commanding officer, and by 1965 the rank of lieutenant-colonel.

He was knighted in 1983 and in the same year appointed to the Queen's bench in the High Court. He was made Honorary Colonel of the 21st SAS Regiment. In 1991, Macpherson was appointed an honorary fellow at Trinity College, Oxford. Throughout his legal career he was involved in many important cases, including the conviction of the serial killer, Robert Black, in 1994. He retired in 1996. In 1997, Macpherson was appointed head of the inquiry into the murder of Stephen Lawrence. They published the inquiry in February 1999 which became known as the Macpherson Report. The report, in which he made over seventy recommendations, has been called:

'One of the most important moments in the modern history of criminal justice in Britain.'

The third judge to sit in on my case was Peter John Gower, QC. I don't know much about this man, and there is little online to help. He was called to the bar in 1985 and took silk in 2016. He was appointed as a recorder in 2017. He had been criticised in the *Telegraph* for dishing out too lenient a sentence of only 4 years to Roy Whiting for abducting and sexually assaulting a girl, five years before he murdered Sarah Payne, God bless her soul.

Gower described the criticism aimed at him after Whiting's sentence as "water off a duck's back." His father had been a respected judge too, famous for once calling Laurence Olivier as a witness in a case.

So, you can now see the judges who I stood before in the Royal Courts. All powerful and intelligent men, who knew the law of the land like the back of their hands. It may also be of importance to note that each judge retired or resigned in the same year they acquitted me!

It is difficult to recount exact speeches that went back and forth over the first few days. They took me back to Brixton every teatime and brought me back to the court every morning early, ready to see out the next day's arguing and deliberating. It was all very stressful, and I slept like a log on a night through sheer mental exhaustion back in the prison.

On the fourth day, there was some slight confusion as we were delayed setting off. The prison had received information regarding another IRA bomb that had been planted in a phone box just down the road from the High Court. It was a strange feeling wondering about these bombs, because this was the second now within a week, and I felt I was right on top of the locations. As the van left from Brixton that morning, snaking its way through the dense London commuter traffic, not so far away, and on my route that the van would normally take, a 5lb IRA Semtex bomb was being disarmed in a telephone box on Charring Cross Road, which is just up the road from the Courts of Appeal. They had informed the van of the huge operation by the bomb squad to dismantle it and cleared the area for safety reasons. So we came in another way to the courts.

The van eventually took a different route towards the Strand and after being processed in to the cells, I was soon standing next to the Rat up on our balcony looking over and listening intently to the three judges and my QC, Rodney Jameson down below, who was fighting the case very well indeed. The judges adjourned for lunch, and Rodney came down to the cells and said to me he thought it was going well. It was hopeful to hear this, but I couldn't quite shift the doubt that we were going to continue to get stitched up and that this living nightmare would continue on for the next decade in prison. Around a week before I had left HMP Liverpool, I had received an official slip of paper under my cell door explaining that I had been allocated to HMP Wakefield and I would be relocated to this prison as soon as cell space became available!

On this particular lunch time, the cells must have been quite full, and the court guards had put me and the Rat in with these two older chaps, who had serious gangster written across their faces. They were sound with us though, offering a few sandwiches from their plentiful supply that they had made up themselves. They listened to our case and said it sounded a right load of old pony. These cockneys were the real deal and said they had only come for a day out from HMP Parkhurst, because they knew they had no chance regarding their own appeal. They had beaten a man severely years ago and broken his arm and ribs and left him pretty much for dead. But this guy who they had beaten had also been under arrest too, and after receiving extensive help at the hospital, had been put back into police custody. The bloke had died in custody that night, and they had found the two blokes in the cell with us guilty of murder. They had denied this at court and even had a doctor say that the injured man was in a bad way but was not suffering from any life-threatening injuries. The two blokes claimed that the old bill had killed this bloke in custody and conveniently blamed the pair of them. I've no idea whatever happened to them both, but I believed their story as they believed mine.

After lunch they took us back up the long flight of wooden stairs and we stood once again while the three high judges strolled in with full bellies. There seemed to be an atmospheric change in the air after lunch, and by the time the afternoon came around I was watching and listening carefully to Lord Staughton who suddenly picked up a huge red leather bound law book which seemed to have a page marked ready for him to read from. He looked up at me and held my gaze for a moment before looking down and reading a short passage from this book. He then said,

"And you are free to go."

Chapter 26

It seemed as simple as that! The guard nudged me out of my daze.

I said to him, "Am I free?"
To which he replied, "It looks like it, mate."

I looked down to see my QC smiling and nodding his thanks at the three big-wigs and then he turned sharply from his spot and with his black silk gowns flying he strode like a winner down the corridor towards the back of the room. The Rat was smiling, and I felt like a weight had been instantly lifted from my tired shoulders. We bounced like children running down the stairs on Christmas Day to see what Santa has left, and as we got back to the cells, we shouted our good news to the Parkhurst gangsters, and they whooped and hollered in our joy as well.

I remember the court guard saying he would have to put us back in our cells while they did all the necessary paperwork to release us officially. He went to shut the cell door, and I stuck my foot in the way and told him he could leave that open now, which in fairness he did.

I just sat there in shock on the little cell bench, not speaking. The Rat was the same. The pair of us were just soaking up the feeling of freedom again, and that this joke of a case seemed to be finally over. The judges, it seemed, didn't need the fifth and final day to decide that they had read and heard enough from my QC to acquit me of the crime of rape.

I should have come out of the front door like you see in the film, *In the Name of the Father*, and had my say into some reporters microphones, but it doesn't work that way and I guess a lot of motivation to write this important account is to explain this matter.

No one gives a toss about the average man on the street. It's only if you have served decades and have received massive news coverage, that you will come out and be able to tell the world just what a nightmare miscarriage of justice you have been subjected too. The Rat made sure we didn't come out the front door anyhow, as he was worried about being gate arrested by Detective Mc DX, who like I mentioned, had been sitting patiently at the back throughout the trial. The question is, why was he worried about being arrested? Had the police not been able to speak to him in length at Doncaster prison when he had left the wing to go see them?

So we snuck out the back door, hiding like idiots, when I should have been at the front door screaming to the world what had just happened to me. Again in hindsight, if I'd known then what the Rat's secret was, I would have cut ties with him there and then and gone out the front doors alone.

The capital city seemed like it was in fast-forward motion to me. Even though the bomb which they defused earlier had put the capitol's regulars and tourists on the back foot, to me it seemed like everything was moving at high-speed. If only you could bottle the joy that being released from prison gives you. Even when you have been guilty and served your time, it's elating. So, I'm sure you readers can only imagine how an innocent man feels when he's just stepped out of the highest courtroom in England. I was buzzing, and every bad thought and feeling right then drained from my body. It amazed me at the normal things we just take for granted. Before getting a bite to eat, we wanted to store the clear plastic prison bags that had HMP stencilled in huge letters on its side. So, by dumping this obvious stigmatic sign we were carrying, we would get back some of our much lost dignity.

We headed toward Kings Cross Station to see if we could store the bags in a locker. Old Bill was everywhere near the station, and we went and asked this train guard where we could put our bags. The escalator, which again is a novelty when you have been banged up a couple of years, took us down to where lost property was and there we asked the geezer in charge how we could store our bags. Not a cat in hell's chance! The whole station was on red alert and they were not allowing any baggage to be stored or left unattended at all. So we went to Burger King, we would just have to drag our prison bags along.

I bit into my cheeseburger and slurped on my Coca-Cola while picking at salted fries and thinking of the apple pie dessert to follow. It was bliss eating food again for its pleasurable taste. Half an hour later and we needed a solid drink. We found the nearest boozer and got wedged into a corner, while taking turns to go to the bar and bring back pints and whiskies to celebrate. Our train home was something like 10.20 p.m., and before we knew it we were both slightly pissed and relaxed in our snug little corner, and didn't realise we had left it too late to get from where we were to the station in time. At last orders, we got more whiskey and then left the pub and walked to the station, anyway. We wandered down the long platforms and found where our train had departed from and read that the next train back to Wakefield was just before 7 a.m. So we chilled horizontally on these benches and snoozed for a few hours under the train station's mighty lip roof.

We were both wide awake in the early hours and we walked around for a bit to keep warm. Somewhere around 4 a.m. this guard came over and we told him we had just got out and missed the last train. He kindly opened this small waiting room which had these electric heaters inside on full blast. I set my watch alarm and slept on the floor by the heater.

Chapter 27

The beeping on my phone opened my eyes, and I got up and wandered outside the waiting room and went to look at the info screen near where our train was to depart from. Everything looked okay. It said the next train to Wakefield was as we had thought, and it would leave in around half hour. I woke the Rat, and we waited on the bench until the train driver appeared and went aboard to ready the engines. Finally, the doors opened and the few passengers on the platform boarded. As the train pulled out of London, I breathed an enormous sigh of relief. I really felt like I was on my way home. I recall going to the bathroom on the train and looking at myself in the mirror. Jesus, I looked rough compared to the morning they had dragged me from my bed at my uncles. I felt angry, and some bastard should pay for this mistake and the time they had robbed from me.

Stations and stops whizzed by, and finally after a few hours the train driver announced Wakefield Westgate as the next station. It felt weird stepping off the train and walking through the station I knew so well, but now felt so alien. Outside on Westgate, we shook hands, and the Rat got a taxi to Eastmoor, while I walked up towards the Unity Hall building where the local *Wakefield Express* newspaper headquarters is situated. I'd kept a hold of a journalist who had written about the initial arrest and I wanted to tell him face to face that I was free, and that the country's most respected lords and judges had acquitted me.

I entered the reception area to the right and looked over at a long empty desk. I waited a few minutes and then pressed this little buzzer on the desk I assumed summoned some assistance to my enquiry. After pressing it a few more times, this little old lady made an appearance and asked me if she could help. I told her of this journo I was hoping to speak with. When she asked me what it entailed, I replied it's got to do with me being cleared of rape. Her demeanour changed and she went to go try to look for this guy.

I waited another fifteen minutes and then pressed the buzzer a few times. Nothing! I waited like an idiot for another twenty minutes and pressed the buzzer frantically. Still no one came out. I shouted out if anyone could hear me and got no response. I'd been blanked and judged, and I felt it had something to do with the stigma around the word rape. I'd got used to being wrongly judged, by the system first and then by fools in prison who have about two brain cells between the lot of them. But this was a new feeling of disappointment. Hadn't I just said proudly that I'd been released, been *acquitted* for God's sake. I left the building and walked out onto Westgate and the free air, yet in my mind I thought it looked like this battle wasn't over by a long shot, and that now I was going to have to fight another battle to prove my innocence to judgmental fools in society.

It was a huge let-down, and I tried to shrug it off as I got into my own taxi and headed to my mums to see my family. I guess twenty-five years on and still getting abused because of the stigmatic word *rape* was the real push and reason behind me finally writing this story. Again, over a quarter of a century

157

ago, it's difficult to recall exact timelines as in where and what I did first. I know I spent a few weeks in England catching up with friends and family members who had stood by me. My dad had written to me from Abu Dhabi in the United Arab Emirates just before I got released. He had been working there for the past five years; he put it straight forward in ink. I was to fly out ASAP and begin a new life over there living with him, so he could keep an eye on me and try to steer me in a more positive direction. I understood what he meant and even though my mum didn't want to lose me again so soon; she was happy knowing I was away in the sunshine trying to better my life and that I had my dad to watch me like a hawk. As I've stated, I had already reformed myself from when I committed robberies. But this false rape charge and the life it had made me lead for the last few years was just something else. It was going to be difficult to just bounce back, and every so often out of the blue, it would hit me for six and leave me in no doubt that I was mentally damaged.

I sat back, all comfortable in my Emirates airline seat, plugged my earphones into place and switched on one of my favourite tunes. The pilot had just started revving the powerful engines, and the plane flew down the runway.

'EXODUS'

MEN & PEOPLE WILL FIGHT YA DOWN, TELL ME WHY

WHEN YA SEE JAH LIGHT

SO WE GONNA WALK, ALRIGHT, THROUGH THE ROADS OF CREATION

WE'RE THE GENERATION, TELL ME WHY

TROD THROUGH GREAT TRIBULATION

OPEN YOUR EYES

AND LOOK WITHIN

WE KNOW WHERE WE'RE GOING

WE KNOW WHERE WE'RE FROM

WE'RE LEAVING BABYLON

WHERE GOING TO OUR FATHERS LAND

The plane rocketed off the runway and soared away toward the Gods. Once we were above the clouds and the seat belt signs were off, I ordered a few cold beers and munch and sat back chilling with the great Bob Marley singing in my ear.

Chapter 28

I had a great first few months in Abu Dhabi, with my dad finishing work around 2 p.m. and then taking me out to show me around the city, pointing out what had changed since my last visit. I was staying in a lovely villa, with all marble floors and fittings and it had its own bar, where I steadily made my way through case after case of cold beers. I guess even back then you could say it was the start of a bad drinking pattern that would eventually lead me to becoming an alcoholic.

The night life was fantastic, and it was great to be back in the Middle East. I'd spend my days on the beach and my nights moving around the cities many top hotels using their bars to drink and dance with all the other expats who were out there living it up. It had a proper sense of something going on in the air, and I'm glad I spent my time in the United Arab Emirates when I did.

As I've stated, my head was still up my arse. I'd sit looking out at the stunning Arabian Sea, glistening back at me from the hundred degree sun reflecting off its expanse, and think of my prison cell. It was like I couldn't see the beauty in front of me for the dark past, which felt like it was suffocating me. Years later I realised this was the start of the panic attacks and anxiety, and what most would tag you as now as suffering from post traumatic stress disorder. But sat in the splendid surrounding of the Gulf, it was hard to describe right then. I didn't like people behind me and felt, even in swanky nightclub bars, I needed to keep my guard up. It's not until you come out of prison, that you realise you have built a terrific wall around yourself. Inside it's wise to keep a wall of solidness around you for protection, yet outside it was a puzzle to remove the bricks and peep over the parapet without thinking a danger lurked on the other side.

A quick holiday fling, which is what it should have remained, turned into another disastrous adventure for me. I'd met a Norwegian girl down on the beach who was out with her brother visiting their dad who, like my own, worked in the oil field industry. I won't go into too much detail, but we dated and went out to clubs and bars and spent time on the beach and back at the villa for a few weeks. It soon came time for her to leave to finish university back in England. She had been keen to continue the relationship long distance, and on her last night in Abu Dhabi, and for the first time since being released, I explained what had happened to me. As shocked as she was, she believed me and felt only anger at what she knew had been a bad time for me. We were young, early twenties, and I guess I fell in love too quickly. Her belief in me had been what won me over, and I guess I missed being in a relationship after the lonely years in my prison cell.

She flew home, texting me all the way, and we continued talking long distance on the phone for a few weeks. Within those conversations, we ended up agreeing that I would fly back to England and go live at this little cottage she was renting near her university. My dad and a good friend Dan, who I knocked about with in Abu Dhabi, both tried to talk me out of it. I wish in hindsight I'd listened. But I flew from the heat of the Middle East to the rainy skies of Manchester and from there jumped on a train and headed towards this girl's home.

One day, a few weeks later, sat in a quiet pub she turned to me and said we should get married. It was all so sudden and felt unreal. But we booked a date in the local town hall and a few weeks after that we were man and wife. She finished her degree and then asked me if I would move back to her home country of Norway, so she could get a better job with her recent qualifications. She had friends who attended Harvard University in America, and as I was dreaming of becoming a serious writer, it all just seemed to fit my new world. It seemed a long way from Brixton prison.

So, we flew to Stavanger, and we moved in with her mother while we looked for a place of our own. She soon got a job and I just kinda drifted around the city, finding my way, and trying to secure some employment. It was hard though, as I didn't speak the language. We found our own place to live on Crystal Street, and everything seemed okay for a few months.

I then came home one day to find her locked in the bathroom. After numerous pleas for her to open the door, as I felt there was something seriously wrong, I forced it open and found she had cut her wrists quite badly. I got her to the hospital, and she got stitched up and we talked about it and I tried to understand where the hell all this had come from. After speaking to her mum, I found out that this was not the first time she had done this. I really tried to help her, but my brain at the time just couldn't handle it. I was too young and too traumatised from what had happened to me to be of any real use. It gave me flashbacks to prison and the people I'd seen cutting themselves. It also put a massive suspicion between us, because whenever I left the house I just felt I'd come home to her cut again.

I finally left on the ferry and returned to Newcastle and then took a train back to Yorkshire, where I stayed with an old friend while I tried to figure out what to do. I spoke to my wife on the phone regularly, but she seemed distant and eventually we agreed I'd go back to Norway on the ferry and try to work things out. It didn't work! And before long I'd returned to England, and we agreed to separate. I think we both realised we were damagcd and that initially we had got along great, but then our problems had surfaced living together and we knew we should have just left it at a holiday romance. I remember phoning my dad back in the Middle East just before I left Norway, asking if I could return. He told me I had made my decision and that I needed to make my own way back in England. I felt let down that he didn't want my return, but again, looking back, I totally understand why he said what he did. I was a drifter; I guess. I didn't know what to do with myself or know where I wanted to live.

Chapter 29

I went back packing around Spain for a while, enjoying being free and discovering cities such as Barcelona. I'd hop on a cheap ferry to Ibiza and then hop on another from there to Palma and then back to Barcelona. I remember taking long bus rides down to Valencia through Inca, and just roaming around without a care in the world. I think now looking back I can see that I didn't know what to do with myself. I'd started writing stuff down in notebooks, poems and song ideas. Years later, again looking back, some stuff that would go into my first novel, *The Ink Run*, was written back then.

I went to Greece for a holiday, and then I went to Barbados. I then got a job working in Portugal for a while and then took a job back in England doing sales that took me all over Scotland, and eventually over the Irish Sea and into Belfast. I loved it out in Ireland and have fond memories working out along the Antrim Coast, where I stayed in a cottage for a while and would walk on a night down to the Giants Causeway and just sit on the huge stone slabs watching the sea smash into them with its spray thrown up into the air.

I'd been offered a job from the Canadian guy I was working sales for, to travel and set up an office in Australia selling maps and globes to schools and universities, but we had a fall out near Dublin and I flew home in a mood and never went.

It was around this time, back in my mother's hometown of Wakefield, that I started going into different solicitors, trying to get some clarity into what I knew was a massive miscarriage of justice. I guess some people might wonder why I didn't go to the solicitors straight after release, but the truth I guess, is that I was too traumatised to deal with opening it all back up right then. I needed to distance myself physically and even more so mentally. But it had always been on my mind to go for compensation, and quite rightly too. The ex gratia payment from the government's coffers was what I was after, and after searching around a few different solicitors in Wakefield, I settled on one on Bond Street and got down to the basics of applying to the Criminal Review Commission for what I felt was owed me.

What price do you put on things such as this? I read through the guidelines from the government and it appeared they owed me hundreds of thousands of pounds just for time spent in my cell. Every day was totalled up, and a figure agreed. Then there was potential loss of earnings, and the most, I felt, the trauma and stigma and hurt caused by the whole sorry episode. It wasn't long before I had my first knock back. The government are great at apologising just enough to mean it, yet the way they word articles, it leaves a lot of red tape and this is how they get around not paying out people like me who have basically been kidnapped by the authorities from their own home and shut away in prisons. I soon had the solicitors appealing this and again waited months to hear that the review of the review was going nowhere. I had a letter direct from the Appeal Judges outlining how and why they had come to their decision of acquitting me.

It was also around this time that I had started drinking heavily around the city centre and smoking a lot of strong weed. The doctor had also placed me on a prescription of sleeping tablets and other tablets for anxiety, because my panic attacks were getting more frequent and severe. I could wake up positive and within the time it took to get out of bed I could have an attack, which would see me hide under the covers and stay there until lunchtime.

Around this time I had received information from the criminal injuries board explaining to me that **MISS LEGALLY ANONYMOUS** was trying to get compensation herself for her injuries! There were no injuries. There had been no rape. But I at least had the perfected grounds of appeal papers, and in the criminal injuries letter they had said I was welcome to attend the hearing and show whatever evidence I felt I possessed to counter her claim. I felt so fucking annoyed that she was getting a hearing in York to be awarded money for injuries, when the only injury she had was a lying bent forked tongue.

I turned a corner near the old bullring in the city centre and by chance bumped into the Rat who stood at the banks cash machine. I told him about the letter, and he said he had also received the same info, but unfortunately he couldn't attend as he had to work. Now, again, I remember arguing the point that this was seriously important and surely he could take the day off to help me stop this absurd claim. He promised he would see what he could do, but I remember leaving him and walking away with a nagging doubt in my mind that I just couldn't put my finger on.

It's again that same old. If only I knew then in hindsight the secret he was keeping from me, then I would have understood his reluctance to attend. I ended up going on the train on my own and making my way towards the minster. I had a map included in the letter to explain which building the hearing was in. It was just behind the minster in these grand looking buildings. I entered the conference room to a full table of seated gentlemen.

I had in my hand the perfected grounds of appeal and I'd read over and over on the train journey the parts where the police surgeon had examined her and found *zero injuries, either internal or upon her outer body!*

From her statement to the criminal injuries board, it was clear she was still trying to push her own agenda to make out she had suffered terribly. I sat and listened while her representative made her case for her. She wasn't there. At one point he said to me in a back and forth argument that I was a convicted rapist! I remember turning to the chairperson in charge of the meeting and telling him this was bang out of order and that I was sick of this stigma and slander, as they had acquitted me in the High Court. I was absolutely furious but conducted myself well and put my evidence proving she had lied through her teeth in court, into the meeting notes.

Once the hearing had concluded, they told me I wouldn't get the information whether she had been successful! Again, I was livid. Detective Mc DX was there and as I left the building, he was standing in front of these double glass doors. I had to summon all my inner strength not to run at him and smash him through them. He spoke to me as I was leaving, and I told him with tears in my eyes from hatred just what he had done to me and that my life was ruined by all this bullshit lies. He told me he believed me, but that he had to do his job. The wanker wished me well, and I got as far as crossing the road and walking away from the buildings and back in front of the minster before I headed into the Guy Fawkes pub to rinse away my fuming anger. It wasn't the best solution, and I soon found myself sinking deeper into dark despair after emptying pot after pot of the dark Guinness. The one constant thought in my mind, was that it was just one slap in the face after another. To think they may pay her out when she is nothing more than a lying piece of shit and a disgrace to genuine victims of rape who deserved that money.

I had taken to sleeping on my bedroom floor like some dog. I was seeing a local psychiatric nurse at my doctor's once a week, and I was descending into a very dark place. In her opinion I was punishing myself for no reason and because I had been living the case for years, I felt imprisoned even though I was free. Looking back it's true, the prison experience was terrible, but it's nothing compared to the mental upheaval I've dealt with since acquittal.

Dealing with the case all the time was just taking its toll on my mental health and I was getting nowhere fast regarding the ex gratia payment. I was getting locked up by the police regularly now for trouble in and around the pubs and being drunk and very disorderly had become a way of life. The police would treat me like shit in the cells, and I gathered they got some kind of sick enjoyment as they watched me descend deeper into alcoholism. When sobered up, I would explain to the judges I needed help and that my offending was stemming from this miscarriage of justice that was wreaking havoc in my head. But no help came. Instead, I would be tagged for community service or bound over to keep the peace.

I'd sold a house that my granddad had left to the family and blown the share of money I had received on drink. The only good thing was a trip out to India, which helped me get into a lifelong love affair with meditation and Buddhism. Back then though, my drinking was too strong for even Buddha to intervene, and I carried on stumbling down my destructive path.

After the last knock back from the crime commission review, where the appeal judges had covered their backs in not slagging off the Crown Court judge, Arthur Hutchinson, even though in my appeal, my QC, Rodney Jameson, who is now Judge Jameson had clearly marked out many incidents within the trial where the Crown Court judge had misdirected the jury and been hostile toward me and my witnesses.

I guess as they all attended the same colleges and universities and would have been on the same social circuits; they would never slag Hutchinson off publicly.

{ PERFECTED GROUNDS OF APPEAL BY JUDGE JAMESON\SHOWING THE CONTRADICTION TO THE APPEAL COURT JUDGES SAYING THERE WHERE

NO ERRORS FROM JUDGE HUTCHINSON!}

HIS HONOUR JUDGE HUTCHINSON, TOLD THE JURY THAT HE DID NOT KNOW IF THE DEFENSE COUNSEL HAD A BETTER KNOWLEDGE OF PSYCHIATRY OR PSYCHOLOGY THEN HE DID, BUT THAT HIS KNOWLEDGE WAS MINIMAL. THE JUDGE DREW ATTENTION TO THE FACT THAT NO EXPERT PSYCHIATRIC OR PSYCHOLOGICAL EVIDENCE HAD BEEN CALLED BY THE DEFENCE. THE EFFECT ON WHAT THE JUDGE SAID WAS TO POUR COLD WATER ON THE HEART OF THE DEFENCE CASE.

THE DEFENCE COULD NOT HAVE CALLED PSYCHIATRIC OR PSYCHOLOGICAL EVIDENCE, IT SEEMS TO ME. WE HAD NO ACCESS TO THE COMPLAINANT (AND WOULD SURELY NOT BE GIVEN ANY)

WE COULD HARDLY HAVE AN EXPERT SIT IN COURT SIT IN COURT JUST IN CASE THE EVIDENCE MIGHT GIVE RISE TO A "PSYCHOLOGICAL" DEFENCE.

THE JUDGES DIRECTIONS WERE UNFAIR. THE POINT IS EVEN STRONGER THAN THAT, BECAUSE DURING THE

TRIAL, MR JAMESON,(FOR HYDE) ASKED FOR LEAVE TO CALL EVIDENCE FROM THE COMPLAINENTS FATHER, AND TO PUT THIS TO THE COMPLAINANT HERSELF, THAT SHE WAS HERSELF THE PRODUCT OF A "ONE NIGHT STAND" AND THAT SHE (AND HER MOTHER) HAD BEEN REJECTED FROM THE OUTSET BY HIM. THE POTENTIAL EFFECT ON THE GIRLS SENSITIVITIES, SEEMS OBVIOUS TO ME.

HOWEVER THE LEARNED JUDGE HUTCHINSON RULED THE EVIDENCE IRRELEVANT, AND THERFORE INADMISSIBLE.

THIS WAS A WRONG DECISION, IN MY OPINION, AND ITS EFFECT WAS TO WEAKEN THE PSYCHOLOGICAL CASE WHICH THE JUDGE FURTHER SCORNED.

IT IS MY OPINION (FOR ONLY THE SECOND TIME IN 16 YEARS PRACTICE) THAT THE VERDICT IS UNSAFE AND UNSATISFACTORY.

THE WAY THAT THE LEARNED JUDGE DEALT WITH THESE MATTERS, UNFAIRLY WEAKENED THE FORCE OF THE DEFENCE COUNSELS SUBMISSIONS.

SO FAR AS THE SUMMING-UP IS CONCERNED AT THE END OF THE TRIAL, I MAKE THE FOLLOWING POINTS.

1. **AFTER AN IMPECCABLE SUMMING-UP OF THE LAW, THE JUDGE COMPLIMENTED THE JURY ON THE CARE THEY HAD TAKEN WITH THE EVIDENCE. HE SUGGESTED THAT AFULL REVIEW OF THE EVIDENCE WAS, THERFORE, UNNECESSARY. HE WOULD THERFORE ONLY REMIND THE OF SOME "MILESTONES" THE REMAINDER OF THE SUMMING-UP TOOK TWO AND A HALF HOURS AND, WHILST NOT IGNORING THE DEFENCE CASE, WAS UNFAIRLY HOSTILE TO THE TWO DEFENDENTS.**

2. ON SPECIFIC POINTS, THE JUDGES COMMENTS AMOUNTED TO MISDIRECTION.

Even when my Mum had come to court to explain that I had told her that I had slept with MISS LEGALLY ANNONYMOUS before, and that my Mum had seen this lock of hair I had shown her, which MISS LEGALLY ANNONYMOUS had given me a few weeks earlier, when I had slept with her for the first time.

Here is what my QC at the time had to say about my Mum at court in his perfected grounds of appeal papers. And I must keep stressing the point that my QC Mr Jameson is now a very well respected crown court judge.

MRS HYDE WAS AN EXCELLENT WITNESS, WHO WAS UTTERLY UNDAMAGED BY CROSS EXAMINATION.

SUMMING –UP

JUDGE HUTCHINSON INVITED THE JURY TO THINK THAT MRS HYDE WAS PROTECTING HER "DARLING BOY"

AN UNATTRACTIVE SLUR WITH NO EVIDENTIAL BASIS.

My Mum would never in a million years have attended court and taken the stand and lied. She was just telling the truth, just like I had done from the very start of this farce of a charge.

Chapter 30

Because of that, I snapped.

I had spent the entire day drinking whiskey in different public houses around the Wakefield city centre, and as dusk fell I started walking in no particular direction out of the city centre. In my drunken state I had no idea where I might have been heading, maybe for fast food, maybe towards my mother's home, I can say for certain though that I wasn't walking toward my own home on Doncaster Road.

As I got to the edge of Clarence Park, I had wondered along the paths that take you past the large duck pond and I recall thinking, I should just throw myself in. I'd had suicidal thoughts for quite some time, but they vanished as quickly as they reared up, and I always got rid of the dark thoughts and tried my best to focus on some good things I felt I still had in my life.

I had started writing a novel titled *The Ink Run*. It was my way of pouring out onto paper some of the deep pain I felt, and it helped me so much. I felt my family too didn't deserve me killing myself, but on this particular night I just couldn't override the urge to just end things. I had had enough of all the bullshit and the stigma of this miscarriage of justice and I moved away from the edge of the pond and walked into the parks rose garden where I knew there were no people about. The park was empty anyway, but I

174

thought if I went to the darkest, most quiet corner, then I could do myself in without disturbance.

I removed my leather belt from my jeans and secured it tightly around my neck and then I reached up while standing on this bench and tied it around a solid branch, and without hesitation I fell forwards. It is devastating to write this now some twenty-five years later. I can't help but think if I had succeeded, then this story for sure wouldn't have been told and I would, in all sadness, just be some suicide statistic. My loved ones and close friends would understand why I had done it, but the stigma vultures would have been out picking over my dead bones, saying I did it out of guilt, which is just too ludicrous to think. It was more than a cry for help, but for me it turned into just that. The branch snapped with my drunken dead weight, and I crashed into the ground. So much for thinking no one would disturb me, as it turned out some dog-walker had seen me and phoned the police, and they were the last people I wanted to see.

They had just come to ask me what I was doing, and although it was pretty obvious, I still didn't get any real concern regarding the gravity of the situation.. It ended up with them taking me up to the hospital and after they had checked me over; I got into an argument with the police about my top. The designer top I had on had, somewhere along the line, been removed and I was being told to leave the hospital without it. Again, I didn't have anyone asking me if I needed to speak with a shrink or if I needed someone to talk to. I was assessed and told I was okay, and to leave. I refused until they found my top, and the police had said I didn't even have a top.

This caused a scene and as I was refusing to leave without my top, this plod came over with some old granddads jumper and said, "Here put this on and shut up." This is an hour after I tried to kill myself. As I've stated, the Wakefield Wood Street police force are scum and treated me in my darkest hour like shit. I ended up verbally abusing the police and getting arrested. So I spent the rest of the early hours in a cell. In the morning they charged me with being drunk and disorderly and gave me a date for court. Again, no mention of any help, or services, for someone, who only a few hours ago, tried to hang himself.

I'd gone to see my MP around this time, Mary Creagh. At first she had listened to my concerns regarding the police and my miscarriage of justice. I even had letters back from her saying she had spoken to the attorney-general on my behalf regarding the ex gratia payment, and they had informed her there was nothing more I could do. She had said if I had a complaint against West Yorkshire police then I could ask for my data they held. This was because of an incident where the police had arrested me for drinking or criminal damage, and in an interview they had left a file on the table when the officers left the room. It was obvious they knew I would look. To my disgust and anger, on the top sheet of my criminal record where all my offences were listed, in bright red marker they had written,

RAPE 10 YEARS!

I had gone ballistic, and the cops had rushed back into the interview suite to calm me down. They had taken the file, and as I sat there fuming; they came back in with one of them carrying the file under his arm. I had said what a piss-take the writing was in the file, and then I knew for sure they were playing fucking head games.

They placed the file on the table and this smug cop flipped it open and I stared at page one of my record. No writing on it. A new sheet, fresh out of the printer, stared back at me. It was for this reason I was in my MP's office wanting to put a complaint in about West Yorkshire police.

I knew I wouldn't get any joy from the MP, or from anyone who I tried to complain to about my treatment. The police, on another arrest, had put me into the cells because they'd booked me for being drunk and disorderly. They had taken my belongings, as they do, and put them into a clear sealed bag. Now, this bag could be any bag as far as I am aware. When I got released and went home, I knew something wasn't right. You know when you can feel someone's been in your home. I looked about and soon noticed a blind in my bedroom had been moved. It was only slight, but I knew how I had my things and it had definitely been opened and then shut again, but they had not shut it quite how I had it. My laptop had also been moved slightly, and when I flipped it open to check it I was stunned to see that the **shift** button had been pulled off and placed on the inbuilt mouse control pad. Call me paranoid, but it was a very subtle message from Wood Street police to me. But I was going fuckin' nowhere and was as determined as ever now to get my life in order and prove what had happened to me in this bullshit rape charge.

The Wakefield Express newspaper wrote a small article in its Friday edition about my suicide attempt. It was highly embarrassing, but in a way it helped me for a while as it clearly stated that I had been acquitted and served time for an offence I didn't commit. It was Kim Foley who represented me in court and had helped me defend my charge. The paper had put clichés of bullshit too, like mud sticks. You can say that again. But it served a purpose, and I left it online for the haters and slanderers to see.

WAKEFIELD EXPRESS

MAN IN TORMENT AFTER FALSE RAPE CONVICTION

A MAN JAILED FOR A SEX CRIME HE DID NOT COMMIT TRIED TO KILL HIMSELF A COURT HEARD. DALE BRENDAN HYDE, 32, WAS JAILED FOR EIGHT YEARS IN 1994 AND SERVED 27 MONTHS IN CUSTODY BEFORE THE COURT OF APPEAL GAVE HIM HIS FREEDOM.

KIM FOLEY, DEFENDING HYDE ON A CHARGE OF DISORDERLY CONDUCT, SAID, "UNFORTUNATELY, MUD STICKS, AND FROM HIS RELEASE DATE TO THE CURRENT DATE, HE HAS EXPERIENCED EXTREME PROBLEMS. HE BEGAN DRINKING IN AN ATTEMPT TO TRY AND NUMB HIS FEELINGS"

WAKEFIELD MAGISTARATES HEARD HE HAD SCARS AT THE BACK OF HIS HEAD AND HAD BEEN ASSAULTED NUMEROUS TIMES BECAUSE OF THE ALLEGATION THAT WAS MADE AGAINST HIM IN THE PAST.

LAST MONTH HYDE, OF BUCKHINGHAM COURT, BELLE VUE, PLEADED GUILTY TO DISORDERLY CONDUCT, WHICH TOOK PLACE IN THE ACCIDENT AND EMERGENCY DEPARTMENT OF PINDERFIELDS HOSPITAL ON DECEMBER 15TH.

MRS FOLEY SAID HYDE KNEW DRINKING WAS NOT THE ANSWER BUT HE FELT HE COULD NOT GET AWAY FROM THE WRONGFULL CONVICTION IN 1994.

HE HAS MADE SEVERAL ATTEMPTS TO CLEAR HIS NAME, BUT THEY HAVE FALLEN ON DEAF EARS AND TO SOME HE HIS STILL CLASSED AS A RAPIST.

SHE SAID, "27 MONTHS OF HIS LIFE WERE SERVED FOR AN OFFENCE HE DID NOT COMMIT"

Chapter 31

Relationship wise, I had got myself involved, one after the other, with the worst three women I've ever met in my life, except for **MISS LEGALLY ANONYMOUS.** Looking back, I was in no fit state to be in any relationship, and the hassle and trouble that followed dealing with horrible narcissistic witches is too long and tedious to mention. The only good thing that came out of it was a beautiful son, my only child.

After the years of stigma and slander, I've always known I would write my true account down of all this, so he at least can see what his dad had to face and deal with. It kills me to think he will have to read all this, but I need him to know I'm telling the truth. The evidence is included, so I'm sure he will figure it all out for himself.

The magistrates had continued to put me on tag or community service, instead of doing what I'd pleaded with them to do and help me with my drinking. Without drink in the equation, I committed no petty crimes, yet the court was too stupid to see the obvious, so I went and did it myself. I had continued to attend my mental health nurse sessions, and now I attended Wakefield Alcohol Team (WAT), in St Johns to get counselling for my drinking.

I had relapse after relapse for the first few months, and then one night I had been drinking in my granddads old pub. It had been the Midland Hotel when my Arthur had it, and a rough arse place, and then it had been the same old rough drinking hole as the Roundabout Pub. I was in there when it was the Priory Wine Bar. A place I would often drink, as it was full of posh up their own arse bastards and solicitors who would congregate there after work.

I could feel the hate rising from my bowels and I'm sure they all just thought I was some well-dressed arsehole who needed to get a taxi home and call it a night. I never would though, and it's so embarrassing thinking back to how drunk and angry I must have looked, but they just didn't know what inner turmoil was running through my brain.

On this one night I had spotted Martin Lord, who owns his own solicitors' firm in Wakefield. I'm ok with him now, although I still think he's a little wary of me. But back then I hated him as I felt his solicitor, Julie Allott, had not represented the Rat very well. Again now writing this some twenty-five years later, I find it unlikely to not assume they didn't know of the Rat's secret. Julie knows in her heart I'm no rapist, and she has tried to help me years later when I've needed advice. But on this particular night in the Priory Wine Bar, I'd spotted Mr Lord, and I'd been so livid I'd felt the urge to do something violent to him. I walked out instead, raging in my mind, and staggered up the back lane toward the old magistrate cells. It was another thing I would regularly do on my drunken walkabouts around town. I would often find myself sat near the magistrate court steps or looking at the cell bars that ran along the foot floor level, thinking back to my innocent time trapped in there.

I'd go onwards and end up around the corner outside the shut-down Crown Court, which gave me a view across the road of Wakefield Wood Street police station. On this night I'd looked up at the station, which had mostly shut down as they had opened a new station in Normanton and I could only see the odd light from the offices high in the building where the CPS work out of. The Crown Court had scaffolding all around it, it had been closed for years, and some developer was in the early stages of renovating it. In my drunken pain I got it into my head to climb up on its high sloping roof. When I think back it scares me, as again this might have been the end of this story right there, splattered on the pavement, dead from a drunken fall.

I'd done a little scaffolding work as a young lad, so I steadily climbed up the back part of the Crown Court building. Once I'd got on to the scaffolding boards, I'd gone as far inside as I could so no one could detect me. I knew I was pissed out of my head, but I wouldn't have done this sober. Eventually I got to the roof and went through this plan I had in my head.

I worked my way across the high roof towards the front part of the building; it was a high-angled roof like the roof on a church, which is like an upside down V. It was this area that I had been heading for all along. On the ground I had thought I would work my way up and get to the front part of the roof. It was here where the large, white statue of the lady of justice looked down, judging the city. Being drunk, I thought if I get up on the roof then push it over into the road, it will smash opposite the police station's main entrance. In my crazy mind I thought this would lead to the local *Wakefield Express* newspaper putting me on the front page and from that, I would finally get to tell my side of this bullshit charge that has stigmatised me for years.

It's a lot higher than it looks when you're trying to shimmy up towards that statue. I got about as far as reaching out full stretch to touch it enough to know it wasn't going anywhere with a shove. I got back down, thinking I would go home and get a lump hammer or a sledgehammer and come back and do the deed. When I got home, I fell asleep still fully clothed in a drunken haze and woke in the morning to a fuzzy hangover and flash backs of climbing up the scaffolding. It was this act that made me quit drinking for my pain.

I decided to settle down and get myself cleaned up. I had forgotten all the things I loved as I'd been in such a dark place for so long. Gradually I started my early morning jogs along the river again. I would get up at five and head out until I reached the canal towpaths, I would then set off at a steady pace, running and thinking, trying to unscramble the mess my brain had become. The miles grew as time went on, and one day I carried a heavyweight punch bag a good few mile on my shoulder until I came to this clearing in the forest I'd found. I spent a few days with a spade clearing the area around this solid tree and hung the bag with heavy blue rope. I would then jog from my home down the river, box on the bag for half an hour, and then take a steady walk home to shower. It became a solid routine, and I could feel the years of abuse and drink sweat out of my system and brain.

It was around this time my mum told me of a night out she had had with her friends. They were attending a retirement dinner for a copper named Gerry Dickinson. He was having a leaving do as he was moving from Wakefield CID to Ossett. On this night out, my mum bumped into the senior detective in charge of my case, Detective Mc DX, who I heard got a promotion straight after our conviction. He came over to my mum and offered his hand to shake. My mum refused, and Detective Mc DX said he was sorry and that he was only doing his job and that *he knew I had been telling the truth*. My mum had asked him why had he let me get sent down? To which the bent bastard replied, "Well, it was my job, and I was on her side at the time by law." What a fuckin' wanker he is, and I wished I had shoved him through those glass doors in York!

Chapter 32

I trained my body and mind like a monk for three solid years. The best years of my life up to that point. I couldn't stand any drink or drugs or medication and stuck to a regime that many people might find monotonous, but for me it was key to getting my life and sanity back.

I met a nice woman named Elizabeth, who showed me nothing but kindness. But it was something I didn't know much about. She helped me so much, but like always and even up to this day, I find myself having to explain in detail just what sort of past I've led. It's not like you can just say to a new girlfriend, "Oh yeah, by the way, I was convicted of rape, but I didn't do it!"

Things don't work like that. It's the stigma again that rears its ugly, unwanted head every time I get close to someone. Again, I pushed her away and stayed alone. It was like I just couldn't function in a normal relationship and I didn't feel, deep down, worthy of being loved. I was an emotional wreck and I guess I just shut off to protect myself in some strange way. Yet something massive was about to surface, and I can now explain just what the Rat's big secret was all along!

I would buy my local city's newspaper, the *Wakefield Express*, on a Friday morning like most people in the city. I noticed nothing out of the ordinary on the front page when I paid for it. It wasn't until I'd got its broadsheet laid out on my table, and I was sipping my morning coffee, that I turned to page four and spat my coffee out all over the floor in utter shock. A familiar face stared back at me from the print. The Rat.

I read the article in total horror and knew, once I had worked out the dates, that this was the real reason for me being stitched up.

This is what I read, word for word from the newspaper's headline some thirteen years after I had been acquitted!

Friday, March 24, 2006,

Men get total of 18 years for attack

Pair jailed for woman's brutal rape

Rapists Mr ORANGE and the RAT have been locked up for a total of 18 years for a monstrous attack on a Wakefield woman. The jury took only three hours to decide the men were guilty of rape, buggery, and robbery – nearly 14 years after the brutal assault took place in Wakefield

Mr ORANGE, 34, and The RAT, 30, were branded pitiless and cowardly for their crimes at Leeds Crown Court on Wednesday.

The court heard how the duo pounced on the woman as she walked home after a night out on Westgate in October 1992.

And although the victim reported her horrendous ordeal that night, the case remained unsolved until a breakthrough in forensic science.

The RAT was first arrested in 1996 for the rape but was eliminated from enquiries.

At the time he gave a full police interview in connection with the incident, but during the trial he claimed he couldn't even remember the event taking place.

Police records of his original account have been destroyed.

The RAT told the court, "I was relieved when it was over and done with. I had drawn a line under it and had tried to get on with my life."

The court heard the woman was dragged to wasteland, where she was pinned down and subjected to a "brutal and utterly deliberate" sexual attack.

Prosecutor Jeremy Richardson QC said that after she was raped Mr ORANGE told her "We haven't finished with you yet," and she was held down and raped again.

The victim, who can't be named for legal reasons, said: I was just so petrified, I thought I was going to die."

The men then rifled through her handbag and stole some of its contents. The court heard she managed to escape during the robbery but, as she fled the scene, she heard one of the men shout "You are a prostitute and we paid you for it."

Douglas Hogg, defending Mr ORANGE, said he had thought this was the case and they had discussed payment.

Speaking to Mr ORANGE, of Wakefield, Judge Jennifer Kershaw said: "Your attack was brutal, cowardly, pitiless and disgusting to any right-thinking member of the public. It was you who carried out two acts of rape and one of buggery and, in the course of doing so, you hit the victim in the face and put your hand over her mouth so she could not breath. She thought she was going to die and, indeed, did lose consciousness,"

Mr ORANGE was jailed for 10 years after the jury found him guilty of 2 charges of rape, 1 of buggery, and 1 of robbery.

The RAT, of , Wakefield, was jailed for 8 years. He was found guilty of robbery and 1 charge of rape, and 1 charge of buggery by helping Mr ORANGE commit the offences.

Sentencing The RAT, Judge Kershaw said: "You facilitated Mr ORANGE in the first act of rape and buggery by physically subduing the woman by violence, holding her down, helping turn her over and keeping her there.

"You may have only been 17 at the time but you were the first to hit her. You were a willing and enthusiastic partner."

She added it was The RAT who kicked the woman in the head and waved her underwear around and made mocking remarks.

Speaking after the trial, Det Supt John Parkinson, head of Operation Recall, the team responsible for bringing unsolved cases to court using new DNA techniques, said: "They put her through a terrifying, sordid and humiliating ordeal. For nearly 14 years she has been tortured not only by her own memories of what happened to her but also knowing the men that did this were still out there somewhere. It must have been a horrible feeling which made her

suspicious of every stranger she passed in the street,"

He said the case was one of hundreds of undetected crimes the police were revisiting. The RAT and Mr ORANGE were identified by matching their DNA to swabs taken from the victim.

He said: "People who long thought they had got away with these types of serious crimes can now fear a knock on the door."

BBC 1 will be broadcasting this shocking story in a documentary, _Rapists, The Day of Reckoning_, next Tuesday at 10.35 p.m.

I couldn't believe what the hell I'd just read. It all made sense now. All the little things the Rat had done over the years I was always wary about yet couldn't quite put my finger on, why I'd had some gut feeling that things just didn't add up. I had always dismissed these doubts by thinking we were both being stitched up, which for that offence he was. But he knew what he had got into before our arrest. Why didn't he have the balls or the decency to tell me why the police seemed hell bent on sending us down with zero evidence?

Why didn't the police tell me they believed he had done it before? They should have revealed it to me. I would have approached my trial totally differently if I'd known I was actually standing next to a man the police wanted to question about a rape some fifteen months before. They proved he had done it with DNA evidence years later. They didn't appeal either! Just like his family had refused to help him when my mum had asked for money to contribute with her own to get a barrister QC to represent us down in the High Court! The missing jigsaw piece was finally in my hands.

My jury had come back with a unanimous verdict! Beyond all reasonable doubt! How the fuck did they all agree on that conclusion? They all want to hang their heads in shame for getting this so wrong that week. It cost me twenty-five plus years of pain and misery!

In the Rat's later headlines, I read that he was first questioned about his secret in '96, the year we got out. So I'm assuming that as soon as the police got the opportunity to question him in the station about this, they had done so.

There is no doubt in my mind, or my family or friend's minds, that the police knew just what they were doing to me way back in 1994. They questioned the Rat in Doncaster Prison in 1994, so they must have had a reason to see him.

I feel like such a scapegoat for their ignorance to get the Rat sent down. Their mindset must have been on getting him off the streets. **MISS LEGALLY ANONYMOUS** certainly had help with her statement, and I can only imagine what they said to her about the Rat and the crime that they believed him guilty of. Dominant witness theory is a key factor in why suspects are wrongfully identified. Brian Leslie, a forensic expert in coercive interrogation and interview methods says, "How police approach, question, and vet witnesses can be a critical factor in targeting a specific suspect."

So the police didn't arrest him until after he had been acquitted. Yet they questioned him while he was in Doncaster Prison with me. Why? Why would they want to question him? If it was merely because he was on remand for a rape at the time, then why not question me as well? The woman from the power station ordeal must have given some description. When did the police take his jumper to save and take DNA from which would eventually tie him to the case? He had admitted to me in Doncaster that the police were trying to fit him up for an old rape case, yet he had said rubbish to me about them saying the perp had worn cowboy boots. There must have been a good reason for the police to come all the way to the prison and to only want to speak to him. His DNA was later proved to have been at the scene and on the rape victim, who had the shit beaten out of her. Unlike my case, where it was alleged I had assaulted **MISS LEGALLY ANONYMOUS**, yet she had no injuries.

How quickly was the Rat a suspect? It states in the papers they eliminated him from inquiries in 1996. It also states that at trial he says he can't even remember the incident, yet he also says he just wanted to draw a line under it. I'm not sure here if he's talking about drawing a line under the initial arrest and being eliminated from enquiries. Was anyone else questioned about this rape? Was Mr Orange?

Why were the police at our appeal sat at the back of the High Court? Did they want to arrest him there and then? It says the police arrested him in 1996, so it must have been quite soon after we were acquitted for the police to come asking him about this other case. Why didn't they take a statement off him in HMP Doncaster? Did he refuse to speak to them? Who Knows?

All I know is the police were hot on his tail about this case and once they proved he was on the scene; it took a jury three hours to come back with guilty verdicts. Has the Rat been stitched up twice? The victim's injuries don't look like a nice meeting took place, as they battered her about her face.

Why didn't his parents want to pay for him to appeal in my case? He didn't appeal at all in his other case, he went down and served his time, why?

And why didn't he want to come with me to the tribunal in York to give evidence to stop **Miss Legally Anonymous** getting criminal injuries compo?

All I know is I didn't do a thing to **MISS LEGALLY ANONYMOUS** on the night in question in 1994. Everything in the evidence pointed to no rape taking place, yet I was found guilty.

Chapter 33

I met a nice Czech girl, Jana, who again showed me nothing but respect and kindness. These women were the first friendly people I'd met since the whole miscarriage had started all those years ago. I decided to try harder with Jana and not allow what happened with Elizabeth to re-occur. This time, though, something far bigger than my messed up emotions caused us to split up.

I had spoken with a pal down in Leicester named Andy Topliffe, who had grown up around the gypsy stronghold of Hinckley. Many years back he had run something called Field Rage. It was bare-knuckle fighting in the fields away from prying eyes. It was rough and ready, and definitely not for the fainthearted.

He had spoken to me on the phone about a new idea he was having. I'd been part of a group of men on Facebook involved in a page called RAGE, which was run by a good man named Tony Cooks, who is no longer on this mortal coil, RIP. Tony had wanted a no hassle group, but with the online testosterone flowing off the chart and some Irish lads giving him hassle and threats, he ditched the group. I'd seen that Andy joined this group a few months before it folded and just like most, I found him to be a rough and ready no nonsense fella who had a major passion for old style, bare-knuckle boxing. He started his own Facebook page called BBAD. It stood for Bare-knuckle/Broken knuckle and Dustups.

Most of the RAGE lads joined BBAD, and the group grew rapidly. Andy made me an admin with Pete Montgomery, himself, and Clare Monaghan, and we grew the group to ten thousand members. Away from the group offline, me and Andy spoke often about getting a fight night organised. There were many lads online giving it the billy big balls, but they mostly bottled it when we got them on the phone to consider actually fighting.

Andy had three definite fighters from up his way in Leicester, with one lad agreeing to travel down from the Welsh valleys. So, Andy had me sort out the match-ups from Yorkshire. We had one Doncaster lad, Matt, who was keen as mustard, but I'd seen him in the gym and while he had the heart of a lion, he was rusty as an old iron left out in the rain. But we couldn't talk him out of fighting, so he was in. We decided I would fight him as I had been out of the fight game for many, many years myself. In my mind I thought if I could beat him then he would leave the fighting alone. People don't understand the very beginning of BBAD. We didn't know what we were doing really, as we were just winging it. We needed fighters up for bare-knuckle who walked the walk and not just talked a good game on the BBAD online page. Andy said he had a decent fighter and he wanted me to find a solid opponent.

In Dave Radford's book, *Blood is Only Red Sweat*, I got a few mentions, but Nick Towel would tell you himself, that when he wrote it he didn't quite have all the facts. It was me who brought Dave Radford into BBAD Promotions. I think without this move in all honesty, the scene in 2020 would not be what it is today.

I had walked past a pub I knew in Wakefield's Kirkgate, called the Harewood Arms. I popped in for a Guinness or two. The pub looked quite empty and a bloke I didn't know was behind the bar serving. I ordered my Guinness and offered him one on me too. So we stood supping our pints and got chatting about boxing. I could tell Dave was a fighter through and through. His face was marked up like an old pro. I got to telling him about BBAD and he started telling me he had been on the bare-knuckle scene a few years back but had lost touch with what was going on. From behind the bar he brought out a replica boxing belt like the one that Roberto 'hands of stone' Duran had won. It turned out that when Dave had been a top ten pro, he had fought Roberto out in Hammanskraal, South Africa and had taken the legend to a win on points for Duran. Duran lost a title attempt two fights later against William Joppy.

On this belt that Dave showed me, Roberto had written upon it in black marker pen,

DAVE YOU HURT ME IN AFRICA LOVE ROBERTO

So I knew I'd found my man to fight Andy Topliffe's hot prospect for the first BBAD show in Leicester.

I stayed in touch with Dave and started training at his gym in Hemsworth, the Alpha. From here I got Andy on the phone to Dave and we ironed out the details and we were all set to rock-and-roll. The venue was a dodgy, run-down looking club called the

F Bar just out from Leicester City centre. On the arranged day, a few cars set off from the George and Dragon pub in Hemsworth, and we bombed down the motorway in Audis and Range Rovers, buzzin' for the fights to come. Even Dave said when we found the F Bar that it looked well dodgy. It was like the film *Snatch* with Brad Pitt, where the director Guy Ritchie shone a light on illegal fights and gave viewers a glimpse into another world.

If you look up 'BBAD 1' on YouTube, you can view the start of the re-emergence of this gentleman's sport back into the twentieth century. Both Dave Radford and I won our fights, and we returned to Yorkshire in great spirits. Our referee had been Tyrone, the son of legendary middleweight bare-knuckle boxing champion, Paddy Monaghan. Paddy had been the man who had helped Muhammad Ali get his boxing licence back when Ali had refused to go to Vietnam. Also at the first event was grand master Samuel Kwok, who was trained by the legend Ip Man's brother Ip Ching. Grand Master Kwok has serious connections to the legendary Bruce Lee.

After the first event, Andy Topliffe was keen to get the second show sorted. We were all back in Leicester again, but at a better venue called Harry's Bar in the centre of town. It was Halloween and this time I refereed the first fight of the night and was also asked to ref the main fight, Dave Radford v McCrory. I declined because I thought it might look biased as I was rooting all the way for Dave to win. Dave lost in a shock victory for a tough lad in McCrory. Both Dave's eyes were shut, and he just couldn't continue fighting blind, even though he had wanted to.

It was all going great with the new promotion, and it was attracting a lot of attention with the mainstream newspapers, and I was thinking I needed to prove a point and fight someone more dangerous.

I certainly got what I asked for, but it wasn't an opponent I had imagined.

Chapter 34

For months I'd noticed little smears of blood when I had wiped myself after going to the toilet. I just didn't think too much about it back then. If anything, I thought it may be a mild case of piles. I would think back to the years of sitting on cold, stone cell floors and I convinced myself that it was this. Over a few months the blood on the toilet paper would only be noticeable sometimes, and other times it looked quite bad. I had also noticed that there were bloody streaks in the stools. So, I arranged an appointment at my local GP surgery and went along for a check-up. The doctor asked his questions and examined me internally, looking for signs of piles. He found nothing and didn't refer me onto anywhere else. I went home relieved and tried to put it out of my mind. I wondered if I had just bled through straining when I went to the loo.

Around two weeks later, Jana invited me to a big house where some of her friends from Karvina lived. It wasn't a big party or anything, more a gathering for some nice Czech food and a good drink and chat. Most of her friends spoke good English and the ones that didn't, she would just translate for me. Just before we were leaving my house, I felt a terrible stomach-ache come on and I felt like I had the runs. I excused myself and asked Jana to wait for me outside while I nipped to the loo. It came out like the runs and it annoyed me as I had felt well ten minutes earlier. It shocked me to see the toilet tissue full of bright red blood. As you do, I looked down into the pan, wondering where the hell this sudden bout of diarrhoea had exploded from. I was expecting to see a mess and flush it away, but I stared down in horror at a toilet basin full of bright red blood. It was so bad it looked like a chicken had had its neck slashed like in some voodoo ritual. I felt sheer panic but thought to just clean myself up the best I could and go to the party. Before flushing the toilet, I took a photo and when I came out of the main door, Jana asked me what the matter was, as I had looked worried as I came out. I showed her the photo, and she wanted me to go to hospital ASAP. It was a Saturday night though, and I told her I would go to the party and attend A&E the next morning when it would be Sunday and much quieter.

Under the circumstances, I was fairly quiet at the party and left quite early. The next morning I went up to Pinderfields Hospital in Wakefield and checked into reception. The NHS are fantastic at seeing people and I was soon in a cubicle having all sorts of tests done. I don't think anyone likes getting poked and prodded, but I didn't mind as I wanted to know just what the hell was going on in my body. After hours of tests, most of which had something to do with my stomach, as I'd told the doctor that it could be bleeding from my stomach as I'd been sparring at the gym doing some boxing on the Friday morning. I'd had a few worries in the gym as I'd sparred with a few lads. Punches to my stomach had hurt me more than I thought they should do, and they had winded me a few times without much of a shot at all to the abdomen.

So the doctor was looking for signs of internal bleeding, but then the tests came back that my stomach was fine. I was then referred to another hospital for a colonoscopy. They put a camera inside my back passage to check my bowel area on a much clearer scale. I wasn't too worried and just took things easy at home instead of going to the gym. On a work level, I had already started serious work on my epic novel *The Ink Run*, and I think I was about fifty thousand words into the type. It was a book I had handwritten over my dark years, and I was pleased to be working on it again and was looking forward to getting it published.

The colonoscopy was at Pontefract Hospital, a historic market town a few miles out of Wakefield. I was nervous for this test; I'd had nothing like this done before. I thought it was bad enough the GP sticking his finger up my bum, so this long pipe with a camera attached was a proper concern. The embarrassment isn't great either. While getting undressed the doctor doing the procedure asked me to lie on my side and hug my knees into my chest. I had some sedation in the back of my hand via an IV, so I didn't feel pain, just mild discomfort. The doctor was watching this screen I was looking at too, it fascinated me to see my inners. After no more than ten minutes, the doctor said, "Oh", and I heard enough concern to mumble if everything was okay? He said he had seen enough and that he was going to finish the procedure and get me up.

After I dressed and was a little steadier on my feet, he asked me if anyone was with me, to which I replied my mum had brought me and was waiting outside. He took me back to my mum in the waiting room and then asked if it was okay to have a word with us both in a private room. I felt the nerves and knew something bad was wrong, but I wasn't prepared for what I was about to be told.

"We need to run a biopsy test on a piece of bowel we removed while doing the colonoscopy, we don't want to worry you by saying cancer, but we need to prepare you for the worst-case scenario."

My head spun, I couldn't believe what I was hearing, and I walked out of the hospital with my mum, in a state of shock.

Within a few days they called me back, and I sat facing the doctor, who to be fair, didn't beat around the bush and just told me straight he had found a massive tumour in my bowel and it was cancer.

Now, it's true when you get bad news like this that the room spins, and even though mouths are moving and the doctor was speaking, you just can't seem to hear a thing. It was like everything just went into super slow motion. I came out to tell my mum, and the doctor had a reassuring word before we left, saying that they would do everything possible to get me well again.

Within weeks I was on my way to Dewsbury Hospital for consultation. I'd seen a colonoscopy nurse who would be on my care team throughout. They went through what could potentially happen in the surgery I was about to have and explained I would probably need a colostomy bag after the op. My world just seemed to close in around me so rapidly. I'd spent the last few years getting fit in my mind and body, and now I just couldn't believe what was happening to me. It was, I'm sure, the years of stress and all the drinking and not looking after myself because of the miscarriage of justice that had caused all this now.

I was soon on my way to theatre to have this tumour in my bowel removed. The surgery and five-night hospital stay went well, and the surgeon said he was confident that he had removed everything that was concerning him. I was lucky too that I didn't need a colostomy bag, thank God. I was in a lot of pain in my abdomen area but went home and rested the best I could, with my girlfriend at the time looking after me, along with my family.

Everyone was still in shock that I'd got cancer and we were all hoping that now the surgery had gone well, I'd soon be on the mend. They had told me though, that after the surgery I would need three months of chemotherapy in tablet form to help make sure the surgery was a complete success. They call it a mop up chemo, and I'd not been looking forward to more of my body wasting away as I'd not been able to train properly for months now.

A few weeks after I'd had more CT and MRI scans, I was on my way to Dewsbury Hospital with my mum and sister to pick up this prescription from my oncologist to get started on these chemo tablets. I'd thought I was only nipping in to pick up a prescription, so I had told my mum and sister to wait in the car. In the oncologist's office, I sat and listened as he flicked through my file and scrolled down the computer screen. I then heard him say that I should be getting my Hickman line fitted soon at Pinderfields Hospital! He had lost me at this point in the conversation, and I asked him what it was he was on about. I could tell from his face he assumed I knew just what he was on about, which I didn't.

When he said that I would need the Hickman line as I'd be needing six months of intense chemotherapy as the spread to my liver was severe, the whole room just spun again. Again, I could see him talking, but I couldn't digest the words. I looked over at this nurse sitting in the corner of the room and it felt like I was floating. After what seemed like minutes, I said, "Spread?" His reply was that my cancer had now spread from my bowel to my liver and that I had eight tumours scattered all over it. I left his office in a state of shock and floated down the corridor and left the hospital. When I opened the car door, my mum and sister asked if everything was alright, and I just said, "No, not at all," and explained just what had happened.

I won't go into the ins and outs of having chemotherapy, but let's just say it wrecks your mind and body. I went from sixteen stone to eleven in a matter of six months, and I've never felt as close to death's door in my life. I lost all feeling in my fingers and I couldn't feel my left foot at all. Then, I started sleeping at the side of the toilet because being sick was that frequent; the sickness was that bad. I had blisters and ulcers in my mouth, and even when I'd sleep for a full day, upon waking, I would be shattered. So, the bare-knuckle scene vanished into the rear-view mirror, as did my novel, as I just couldn't concentrate to write. Just after I had the

Hickman line fitted, I had flown to Poland and then driven over the border to spend time with Jana's family in Karvina. It was a beautiful country, and they made me feel very welcome, but I was in agony and worrying about what was on the horizon. So, just after my return to England, we agreed it was for the best to split up. I didn't feel it was fair to drag her through this, looking after me. She was a lot younger than me, and I felt it was a massive weight I was carrying, and I wanted to be alone. We remain friends though to this day; she is married now with a family of her own and living back in her own country. So it all worked out for the best.

Chapter 35

The bad news regarding my liver was that some tumours were over certain blood vessels, and if the chemo didn't shift them, then there wasn't a realistic chance of removing them safely. It was all getting very serious in the multi-team meetings. I'd heard, regarding survival chances without surgery, that I was looking at around four months left to live and that the palliative care team would be taking over my case. So, I did the chemo and toughed it out. I thought positively, and only occasionally felt the sheer dread that I might be about to die soon. I just couldn't imagine me being dead, and I kept my chin up the best I could. It's true that saying, *you don't know how tough you are until being tough is your only choice.* I know my own inner strength and it's a solid mechanism.

As an example of just how much it slowed me down, I'd written and typed up fifty thousand words in two months before the bowel cancer diagnosis. In the year since that surgery and getting into the end of the chemo, I had typed only a further ten thousand words. I guess I was lucky to even type anything under the circumstances.

But I just felt frustrated to hell. I had finally got my act together, work wise and physically for this to just now grind me to a standstill. All the training and muscles I'd developed withered away, and it was very depressing. Good news came after some more scans, which were to see how the chemo was hopefully killing the liver tumours. The whole right side had cleared up, which was fantastic news, as this had been where the blood vessels were compromised. So I was green lit for major liver surgery. It's funny how you wish and pray for someone to rip half your liver out! I was under a new surgical team at St James Hospital in Leeds, which was lucky too, as it's the best liver hospital in the country and it was right on my doorstep.

I was very nervous about this surgery and I'd watched live liver resections on YouTube, which wasn't my best idea, but I needed to know what was about to happen to me. I spent ten days in hospital this time in Leeds, St James, with the first few days after surgery in intensive care. It was the second time I'd been in intensive care in a year, as I'd spent a night in there after the first bowel resection. The pain of having half your liver removed is intense. They had removed the whole left side along with my gall bladder and all my lymph nodes to cut down on the chance of the cancer spreading any further. The pain that I felt when I woke from my eight hour operation, I can only describe as what I would imagine being run through by a broadsword on some ancient battlefield would feel like. The scar from my solar plexus to my belly button and then across the bottom of my right side indicates the severity.

I got home though and was laid up in bed again, just trying to recuperate the best and quickest I could. I had to have the initial three month chemo mop up tablets now, which is what I thought I was going for at Dewsbury Hospital just before I found out the cancer had spread to my liver. I lost more weight and puked nonstop for three months. It was a very tough time on my body and mind.

After two years of scans, which were every three months for the first year and then every six months in the second year, my scans looked okay. Well, okay, compared to loads of tumours scattered all over my liver. The surgeon had found a small shadow in my right lung and there was still a small tumour on my liver, but nothing for them to be thinking surgery or chemo about. So I felt I might have just put it all behind me.

In the two years recovering from the liver surgery, I had finished my masterpiece of one hundred and fifty-six thousand words. *The Ink Run* was published to rave reviews. The book was in Waterstones on the shelves next to Stephen King and I felt proud of my achievement, as it had been a mental slog to complete under these medical conditions.

I'd got involved with another woman too, who was a successful business-woman, and she gave me lots of care and encouragement to get myself back up on my feet. I'd also gone and rescued a beautiful Italian war dog who I named Little Nap. This gorgeous Cane Corso was another step in the right direction for my recovery as walking him got me out of the house. I had needed an incentive, even though I was on the mend, the last three years of invasive surgery and chemo had wrecked me physically and I still had many days where I couldn't move much.

Again, in life you just never know what's around the corner and a few months after getting my rescue pup, I went for a routine scan and got the worst news ever. My cancer had spread again, and it was back in my liver with five tumours showing up on my MRI scans. I was devastated and felt at this point that I was going to die. It just wouldn't leave me alone, and I couldn't see a way of ever getting well again.

My family, and girlfriend, Ruth, thought that maybe it was best that I gave the dog up for adoption as I had a huge mountain to climb again, but I couldn't send him back. I loved him so much, and he had been abused before I'd got him, and I felt so protective over him. I decided I would keep him, however difficult things got.

So, I went into St James Hospital again and this time had thirty-five per cent of my liver cut out and ablation therapy, which is where they stick steel rods down directly into the tumours and electrocute them. Again, I was in Leeds Hospital for over ten days recovering. There's so many tubes and wires sticking out of the body on a procedure like this that it's so hard to lay comfortably and rest. It's intensive care for a few days and then doped up to the eyeballs on morphine until you can crawl out of bed and shower, and then you can go home. I spent another three months, mostly bed bound, while I healed from the deep cutting surgery.

I'd struggle with taking the dog out the back of my apartment and feel so guilty as he would look at me as if to say, "Come on let's go for a long walk." But he motivated me like I knew he would, and I started taking small walks with him and before long I was back to where I had been before the cancer came back. The hospital and surgeons and oncologist were adamant that I needed to do another chemotherapy course, as they worried about how the cancer had spread and just how many tumours I'd had.

I've never been a fan of a pharmaceutical approach to curing the body, and the chemo I'd had before, had been a terrible experience. The thing is, it scares and confuses you when you get hit with a cancer diagnosis that you feel you must follow the advice of the doctors in charge. In the years I had suffered with the big C, I had researched so much about the human body and I'd tried many different approaches to healing. From diets and juicing to fasting and meditating, I found that I needed so much more to get me through this successfully, than just what the operations and chemo could do.

So I turned down the chemotherapy that the hospital recommended and went out and sourced pure cannabis oil. It was a hard decision, as I knew that if I got this wrong, it could be curtains for me. I believed in what I was doing though, and the major research I had done on just what benefits pure cannabis oil could have on cancer diagnosis.

So I started a course which would see me build up in the first thirty days to where I could consume a full gram a day. It was a trippy time, and I'd sleep for long periods, and it was this rest that helped the body heal from the invasive traumas. I was doing some deep thinking too, which only helped me more in my studies on Buddhism and the Zen way of life. I then spent the next sixty days taking a full gram of oil every day.

It was a long three months of being off your head and feeling very stoned. It's difficult keeping up that amount, and again I used my inner strength to push through the dosage and will myself to heal. The next set of scans I had came back clear!

I've been clear again now for two years, and I'm just about to have my scans to see how things are looking. In those two years I've been on a positive note, done a hell of a lot more writing.

I published a short story titled *The Whiskey Pool.* It's a self-help book that deals with a fictional story of rebirth and Buddhism. It's a warning for alcoholics too. Like most of my writing, it's awash with autobiographical images close to my own life and past.

I was on my own again now too, as far as relationships went. Ruth had been such a support to me while I had suffered set back after set back with my cancer, but we just didn't work out as a couple. She has my respect always though, and I wish her all the best in her future as she is a very kind soul.

I knuckled down and published a poetry book titled *The Gods R Watching.* I did it while I was working on another major novel. I felt that I needed a few more books out there under my name to go alongside my debut *The Ink Run,* while I worked on this serial killer psychological thriller set out in Texas. I had written thirty thousand words on *The Death Row Thrift Shop* **novel** when I got an offer to write a biography for a friend, Chris Burton. So, I put the second novel on the back burner and started writing *Easy Target.* It's a fascinating true account that has all the elements of a James Bond spy thriller. It's a financial look into the darker side of life in Tenerife, where some of the world's biggest gangsters sit side by side with Chris and his father.

Unfortunately for me, I was half-way through the book when Chris got made bankrupt in a case in the High Courts in London for over six million pounds. It has put the book out of being completed.

So, while the lockdown has been on in the UK with this COVID-19 virus, I had a good long think about getting *The Death Row Thrift Shop* novel finished, but then I thought about this book you're reading now. I have tried to write *Stitched* a few times, and to be honest it has always made me feel down, and remembering such a painful, frustrating time wasn't easy. Yet the stigma I have dealt with for over twenty-five years has urged me on to get it written down. I've had many people slag me off about this charge. Many people don't even realise I was acquitted. But it's been while I've tried to turn my life around that I've been surprised and disappointed in the character assassination that I've endured online. I've got to be visible online as an author, and while I've had so many positive encounters online, I've had my fair share of idiots slandering me.

Chapter 36

I've had one person defame, stalk, and harass me for over three full years. This person is your classic narcissist, who tries to convince the few followers he has that I'm jealous of the books he's writing. The people he writes about are gangsters, mostly dead ones. They have inbuilt followings, and so he has sold a few copies here and there off the strength of the subject's name. It's not his writing skills that sell the copies. This person was and still is a no one, but he came out of nowhere about three years ago and approached the publishers I had my hard back and paperback debut published on. It was only a small publisher, but they offered to help publish my book early on and I thought it would be a good way to at least get it out there, and then I could progress to a bigger company. In hindsight, I should have stuck to my bigger aspirations and chased after one of the proper publishing companies. I'd had some feedback from Canongate before I went with them.

I had helped this novice writer with his very first book, which he had even given me special thanks in the book's front inner page for the help I'd given!. I was quite proud for him that the book hit the number one spot in the boxing charts. But this is where he then started slandering me. He will tell you he's an Amazon bestselling author, which is only true if you get a high ranking in a certain category. It's like the boxing category. His debut might have hit number one, while Tyson's autobiography was at number two, but if you're that naïve to think he sold more books than Mike Tyson's, then you're as thick as the author who wrote it.

I've never been interested in obscure Amazon categories to make out I'm an Amazon bestselling author. My debut book broke into the top 200, 100, 50, but all in categories that such as horror and crime fiction, larger categories than say the categories we might find the few boxing autobiographies in. So, there was never any jealousy at all and never will be.

He must have been looking me up on google search and found the article on my suicide attempt. The article that explained that I had suffered a miscarriage of justice, served time for an offence I didn't commit, that mud sticks, etc. My phone had rung, and Mr YELLOW name flashed up. Like I said, before he started his defamation campaign I'd helped him with his first book. So I answered the phone thinking he would be after a chat about books, but what I got was just a lot of screaming down the phone, shouting at me that I was a dirty nonce and a rapist. I tried my best to shut him up and make him realise he had got it all wrong, but I knew he had also read this info online and I couldn't understand why he didn't understand the words he read. **Acquitted, not guilty, served time for an offence I didn't commit.**

He then started ruining my Amazon reviews on my debut novel. He talks in his narcistic way of me being jealous of him, when really the bloke has an obsession with me and my work. My Amazon reviews were all five stars, right across the board with the most amazing in-depth reviews from readers who had loved my writing skills. Up to present, this

214

bloke and his muppet friends, who are as childish as he is, have put thirty per cent one star reviews on my debut book *The Ink Run* and left reviews like "its dog shit" and " not worth the paper it's written on". I've complained to Amazon, and they have done nothing about it.

I'm quite sure anyone with half a brain cell in their head can read through the fake reviews and still see that my books are well liked and receive good reviews. Their thirty per cent, one star ratings won't ever take away the fact that the real reviews are still seventy per cent, five star ratings.

He doesn't stop there though. He writes slanderous comments under posts I put out on my book pages on Facebook. If I put out an advert for a book of mine, under it he will write written by a rapist or something else. He will spy through my online activity and take a screenshot of a photo and then photo shop it to say rapist. Like, for example, a book's cover I'm showing, he will rewrite over the title Rapey Tales. The bloke is mentally ill and deeply disturbed. Constant phone calls over the years have just got steadily worse. The voice messages he leaves are vile beyond belief, yet he has some of his pals conned into thinking I'm as bad. It's the furthest from the truth that you could get.

I've snapped occasionally and threatened him down the phone but let me explain the circumstances to most who don't realise just what this person is doing. My mobile will ring, I answer, and he will scream many disturbing comments into the phone then hang up. My mobile will ring again a few minutes later, again he's screaming and making weird noises down the phone and doing this weird, disturbing laughter and making threats, then hangs up. He doesn't stop, he phones continuously, even when my mobile is off. When I turn it back on there are threatening messages from him. This goes on for around an hour with up to about thirty calls and five voicemails of utter vileness.

He has gone around telling anyone that will listen that I've threatened his wife and kids. This isn't true at all. I replied angrily once, after one of his hour-long wind ups that he and his family better watch it. But I meant that as in his brothers, father, or uncle.

The truth of the matter is I've got some very serious friends who know all about his disgusting antics and I've had genuine offers for people to drive through from Yorkshire to his home and smash his door down and hurt him in front of his family. I've told these people not to do this as it's not fair on his wife and kid. He doesn't seem to realise just how close he is to being seriously hurt.

He has left voice messages laughing weirdly and asking if I am stressed enough yet? And telling me my cancer will be back soon and I will be dead in a year, then he's going to come and shit on my grave. I have just found out that my cancer has in fact returned, so well done you vile bastard, your wish has come true. I have just completed SABR Radiotherapy to try blast the tumour away again. I would never have thought I could wish cancer on someone, but I hope he gets it in his warped disturbed brain and dies a painful death. This is what I'm dealing with. Let's hope I don't go terminal over his stress and constant slander, or I might do something that I'd normally regret.

I've been to my local police twice now over his slander and harassment. He calls me a grass now to his silly mates because I have done this. I'm no grass, I just have a life these days that is worth protecting and I've come too far to let a stupid bum like him bring me down. The police have done nothing, as he has gone into the police station in tears saying I've threatened him. The second time, the police were going to speak to him again, but I just couldn't be bothered going through with it. I know he's protected by the police for some reason. I even changed my mobile to stop the calls, but he has somehow got it and the abusive calls continue right up to this day.

He even made up a false profile on face book pretending to be me, so he could get mixed into conversations, me abusing my own friends. That's how seriously deranged this idiot is. I got a message off my good friend Dave Radford, who, as I've mentioned in this book, was the man I brought into the BBAD fold of fighters at the start. So, I received a late night message a few months back from Dave saying,

> "I don't duck anyone in the fight world as you know and when I see you, we will see who's a bum!"

As you can imagine, I didn't have a clue what he meant, and I don't take kindly to threats myself and I duck no man either. But I knew this was out of character for Dave, so I sent a message saying,

"What you on about mate?"

I heard nothing back, but then a good pal, Nicky Mallinson, who is very good friends with Dave, sent me a screen shot showing me calling Dave out and calling him a bum fighter in this comment in the middle of a thread post on Facebook. The profile was a photo of me that this bloke had taken off my genuine Facebook account and which he had used to make a false profile.

The name though, was Dale Hyde, not Dale Brendan Hyde. A while later Dave and I spoke on the phone. First, he apologised for sending the message to me in reply to the false message this bloke sent trying to cause me trouble. This immature individual believed that I would end up in a fight with Dave over his nonsense. It's so laughable. I wish he could have heard mine and Dave's conversation about him and this crap. We are fine and will always be pals and share the foundations of a bare-knuckle company that went from fighting in the hay bales in the back of dingy nightclubs and beer gardens, and turning it into a great event at gangster Dave Courtney's back garden in South London, which hit all the national paper headlines and saw us make history that night by putting on the first Atlantic BKB title fight in over a hundred years. The company was later bought from Andy Topliffe and it's now doing regular shows at the 02 in London. Maybe it's this that turns this bloke green with envy. But Dave isn't happy with him, and I'd say it's back-fired in a big way as you don't really want a man like Dave, a bare-knuckle legend being pissed at you for trying to cause trouble with a friend of his.

I'm not the only person this bloke aims his harassment at, as I've had quite a few people message me saying he does it to them. A true narcissist at work, and I hope karma pays him a huge visit one day as the fool is mentally deranged, like a child in a man's body.

.

Chapter 37

There is another matter I want to clear up in this book, and again it's the abuse that I've had to put up with that brought it to my attention. I've had lots of great interviews online, with TV appearances and radio interviews. Some of the best writers in the world have reviewed my work. Their thoughts about the merits of my writing and my ability, and to compare me to some of the best as a writer can be read on online blogs. It's things like this that people read through that cause the jealousy to rear its ugly head.

I've had *Sunday Times* number one best sellers praising my work and giving their blessing for me to use parts of their reviews as front cover quotes on my books in progress, such as Paul Finch and Valerie Keogh. I have already placed great reviews on my debut hard back and paper back by top producer Paul Van Carter, and Penguin bestselling author, Noel Razor Smith.

But this failed author who I call Mr YELLOW started saying things in messages about me raping young girls, and I wondered where he was going with all this. So I checked through a google search under my name, which is **DALE BRENDAN HYDE**, which it has always been. He started saying things about how I've changed my name to hide away from my crimes.

At this point he had lost me, I could understand why he was calling me a rapist, as he had fixated on the online report from the court, which stated I had tried to hang myself and that I had been acquitted. But the nonce references and this changing my name crap had thrown me.

When you type my full name into google, many pages come up with my writing achievements, but if you scroll though until the google search moves away from your original search you will find what I now know this bloke found and what he has used to defame me. The search comes up with a Dale Hyde from St Albans who isn't even me. It states that this person raped a fifteen-year-old girl and then tried to kill himself. I can kinda see where it could be mistaken, but again if you have one brain cell in your head you can work out it's not me.

The source of all of this harassment and defamation, isn't the only person to get this wrong though, and I was shocked when a bestselling writer libelled and abused me online over this same google search that isn't even me.

A former Harper Collins bestselling author and a criminal lawyer to boot, decided one night while drunk out of his skull to plaster across his own Facebook page that I was a nonce! His page is read by many crime readers, and we had hundreds of fellow crime writers as mutual friends. It horrified me when a writing friend messaged me saying, "You best check out what he is putting on his page about you."

For a criminal lawyer, he sure got it very wrong, and I contemplated suing him for slander in court. I still might. What it proved to me though is the pack mentality that comes with online media. There were many comments saying I was a disgusting so and so.

Even when I commented back saying it wasn't me I got verbally attacked.

I sent him a private message and showed him proof of me being at certain events or being on holiday, the sicko would be in prison while I'm on a beach in Mexico for instance, or I'm sat chilling on the beach in Mauritius, or I'm on the Hong Kong ferry sailing over to Kowloon! This sicko from St Albans had also got a clean record. It was his first offence, which again proves this is not me. Unfortunately, I've got a record as long as your arm. He then apologised profusely and put up a statement on his page stating he had been drunk and got it all wrong and that this bloke called Dale Hyde, is not Dale Brendan Hyde the writer.

But the damage was done in my eyes. I should name you really, but I will settle for explaining that I had a quote from a writer in America, who is on fire right now in the publishing world. Mr Shawn A Cosby, whose debut novel was named as one of the best books of 2020 by the New York Times and is getting made into a major film. With Shawn quoting me that my own debut crime thriller **THE INK RUN,** reminded him of **ED BUNKERS, NO BEAST SO FIERCE,** I will in honour of ED, who is considered to be one of Americas greatest crime writers, but who is also well known for playing MR BLUE in QUENTIN TARANTINO'S RESEVOIR DOGS, just call my slanderous lawyer MR BLACK!

And I was further shocked when he told me in a private message, that I have saved just in case anyone pulls me on this issue, that a top female crime writer had confirmed his suspicions when he had asked her. I had already seen her make a comment on line about me being a nonce case, which I confronted her about. All she did was block me.

I won't name her, but she knows who she is, and she disgusts me. My advice to her is, try to get your facts right before slandering innocent people, or I might just sue you as well! To slander me in such a wrongful fashion makes you one dangerous lady!

It's a weird one, that all the people that have helped me, I've more or less named them in this book. Yet the slanderous perjuring pieces of shit and the corrupt police, I've had to resort to giving them made up names. Even now the justice system seems to be on the side of the false tongued, instead of the truthful beautiful people.

Chapter 38

When you come out from behind the gate, after a nightmare miscarriage of justice, there is no help or protection from the system upon release. Why do animals like the Bulger killers or Maxine Carr\Huntley get new identities and protection when they have committed the worst crimes ever, like Mary Bell, all given new identities and re-housed? Me, I got fuck all, and I'd been the victim in the case. It's a disgrace, this system and the courts that supply its verdicts. I've tried over the years to get the media interested, but I've always come back with a blank. I had Sonia Poulton from ITN News Network ask her editors if they were interested, but she said they were not. She agreed to help me with my documentary idea by giving me the interview outside the Royal Courts that I never got back then.

I've contacted a few organisations like Mojo, run by Paddy Hill and I've been in touch with death row exonerees over in Ireland, who run the Sunny Centre as retreats for miscarriage of justice victims to take a break and get their heads back together and find some peace. We are victims, no matter how long or short a sentence you served for nothing. We are part of a unique little club all over the world, and only the members know the pain and suffering that a miscarriage of justice causes to you and your loved ones.

Up to now, all my writing has been influenced by my dark past. Like the quote *Sunday Times* bestselling author of over a million copies sold, Paul Finch gave me:

"His writing has an air of authenticity that other crime writers can only dream of."

Once I've completed the crime book I've left to finish, which is The *Death Row Thrift Shop*, I'm moving away from crime writing for a while. It might sound a bit odd, but I've got some great ideas for children's books and I'm going to work on completing some of them at the end of next year. I will then start work on writing some treatments on my two novels, **THE INK RUN & STITCHED.** I have had many people in the film industry say that both stories would make excellent films or a series on Netflix.

PAUL FINCH SUNDAY TIMES BEST SELLING AUTHOR
Blog spot WALKING IN THE DARK

"At the end of these book reviews, I often like to indulge myself in a bit of fantasy casting, imagining that the book is being adapted for film & TV and nominating those stars who I think would make it live and breathe on screen. I'm not going to do that here for the simple reason that known names would get in the way. If done properly, **THE INK RUN** would be as tough, gritty and unforgiving a piece of cinema as anyone has ever seen, and I suspect that only a cast of unknowns could make that happen effectively (look at KEN LOACH'S movies, if you want the living proof). Even so, I hope it gets made at some point. And if it doesn't hold back, the way Dale Brendan Hyde refuses to hold back on the written page, it would be a major event indeed."

I'm hoping by the Summer of 2021, the last book that I've mentioned, THE DEATH ROW THRIFT SHOP will also be available for purchase. As far as the miscarriage of justice, the case goes on. I've enquired about opening it up with the crime review commission again, stating that my new evidence is the fact that the senior detective in charge believed my co-accused to be responsible for a brutal rape some sixteen months prior to our arrest, and that he was right to pursue the Rat as he was convicted and sent down for the crime some thirteen years later because of advancements in DNA technology. And that he has admitted twice now, once to me and once to my mother, that he knew I was telling the truth. Yet he claimed he had to be on her side as the detective in charge of the case. There is also his diabolical conduct outside the courtroom, regarding him trying to get PC Ward to alter his version of events that night.

I'm sure that my original perfected grounds of appeal by QC Rodney Jameson, who is now an established and respected judge at Leeds Crown Court, and his emailed reply to my correspondence telling me I need a new legal team to help me, and the initial evidence that clearly pointed to my innocence are enough to reopen the case!

What about the obvious discrepancies between the Home Office Justice & Victims Unit, where the letter from Mr Joe Murphy states that the reason I would not receive one penny from the ex gratia payments scheme was because, in short, the Court of Appeal had a *lurking doubt about the safety of your clients conviction!* What fuckin' planet are these muppets living on? A lurking doubt? It's a serious joke that I just don't find the humour in. I have the three High Court Judges letter in my possession, where Lord Staughton states from the official transcription from the official court tape recording, by John Larkin Verbatim Reporters, that in his own words on page 11 of a 13 page report:

"Viewing the case as a whole, there were many factors which cast serious doubt on the truth of Miss Legally Anonymous's account!"

Judge Jameson knows I was stitched up. As I've stated, he has only had two miscarriage of justice cases in his entire career and I'm, in his own words, one of them. He can't help me though, as he is now part of the judiciary. But it's a positive sign when they email you back saying you need to find a new legal team to help. He wouldn't say that if he thought I was barking up the wrong tree, and I'm sure he doesn't forget the frustration he felt as QC back then, and he had to go up in front of such a heavy panel of appeal judges.

Some serious men sat in judgment that day, and even I can recall the way they shot him down and made us all feel like we were mere puppets in their mighty show. They had the experience and common sense to see through the case's total joke status, and even though the Rat had his secret, they couldn't allow two men to serve any more time for a crime that never happened. I feel I'm such a scapegoat in this story, and that's what makes me boil with anger inside.

How dare anyone remove me from my life and put me through sheer hell for nothing? I have in the past, after they knocked my compensation payment claim back and I descended into alcoholism around my city, thought about killing all involved. I know that sounds like I have a screw loose, but back then all this had unravelled all my screws and I was a total mess. I tried to kill myself remember, and as I often contemplated suicide, the thought of getting a gun and shooting everyone who I believed had caused this to happen to me was appealing. If I was going, then we all were. Thankfully, my suicide attempt didn't work, and the branch snapped that night in the park, and I didn't get a gun and murder. But I must be honest and say it came close at times. I'm okay now, after many bumps in the road. Life can be hard when you have such a stigmatic charge hanging over your name.

Some people I spoke with years later, don't even know I was acquitted. The newspapers don't bother writing massive bold headlines when you're released, they just plaster their crap when you're charged and found guilty. I know when I tried to escape the Crown Court, the news agents' shops that have those billboards outside had used our antics to sell more papers. I think they had put on the billboards outside their shops in Leeds for the evening post,

RAPIST PAIR CROWN COURT ESCAPE ATTEMPT!

Or some bullshit like that.

It only took many years after my release, and a suicide attempt, to get a small column in the *Wakefield Express* saying I had served time for a crime I had not committed and been acquitted. To some people that didn't matter, he just used the stigma of the word 'rape' to harass me and slander me for three years.

As much as I despise the RAT and the people involved who allowed this to pass them by and to do nothing to stop this happening to me, I have to, and always will lay the most blame at **MISS LEGALLY ANONYMOUS's** feet. She should be sent to prison for perjury for the full term the law allows for that offence. If you google the answer it says, 7 years. It can be a statement made under oath, such as an affidavit which is made as part of proceedings. This is treated as having been made in a 'judicial proceedings. The maximum penalty for perjury in judicial proceedings is 7 years, which is, I hope what she will one day rightly be sentenced to. And I pray while in there she gets the full force of the system beating her down, just like it brought me to my knees as a young man over her sick lies. Luckily, I'm strong inside, not everyone is, and God Bless to all those incarcerated right now who are innocent and struggling. I hope you make it out soon. And rest in peace to the ones that were not strong enough to make it back into the light. I managed with true grit to stitch myself back together again, and I can only hope this book shines a massive warning light on this stigmatic topic, as it needs addressing in society. I hope I can launch my charity idea of **V. O. I. D.** in time. **Victims of Innocent Damage**.

It would be a charity that I would like to believe would make a difference to victims of these hideous court decisions. Somewhere for people to look towards and see there is help available and advice. It's something that I've searched for over twenty-five years without success. Don't get me wrong, there are many great organisations that help deal with miscarriage out there, but I want V. O. I. D to be for the little man on the street, the forgotten victims that don't have the big media cases. These victims are damaged just as much as those victims in the big infamous cases. Maybe I can stop someone serving years of mental imprisonment on the outside. As for me, that has been the hardest part of this mistaken journey.

The lies even a quarter of a Century later, still sting deep into the heart.

Scorched into the prefrontal cortex (the thinking centre).

Nailed tight to the anterior cingulate (emotion regulation centre).

Tattooed forever upon the amygdala (fear centre).

Peace out.

THE END

Dale Brendan Hyde January 2021

CLARIOR EX IGNIBUS   A LIGHT FORGED IN FIRE

Printed in Great Britain
by Amazon

56657830R00139